THE KIND, FRIENDLY UNIVERSE

Harvey Jackins

RATIONAL ISLAND PUBLISHERS
Seattle

THE KIND, FRIENDLY UNIVERSE

*The cover photograph of Mount Rainier was taken by **Caryn Terri Davis** in June 1995.*

Jackins, Harvey.
    The kind, friendly universe / Harvey Jackins. — 1st ed.
        p.   cm.
    ISBN 1-885357-09-5 — ISBN 1-885357-10-9 (pbk.)
    1. Re-evaluation Counseling.   I. Title.
BF637.C6J322   1995   95-21342
158' .9--dc20

Manufactured in the United States of America

Table of Contents

FOREWORD

The articles in this book have been written in the years 1992-1995.

The world has continued to change rapidly, partially in ways that we would have predicted and partially in ways that have been surprising.

The unsolvable crisis and deterioration of the oppressive society has brought great hardship and suffering to larger and larger numbers of people. On the positive side, this has motivated greater numbers of people to question and begin to reject the society's nonsensical policies. This tottering society brings only illusory benefits to anyone, and these only to smaller and smaller numbers of wealthier and wealthier owning-class people.

The deterioration of the environment continues to accelerate, the extermination of species of living things progresses at a dismaying rate, and the pollution of the oceans begins to rival the pollution of the land.

On the other hand, almost all avenues of human activity, except those directly involved in oppression and exploitation, continue to advance brilliantly. It becomes clearer and clearer to more and more people that humans have the capacity to sustain their beautiful planet and to establish permanent peace and dependable sustenance for a reasonable population. The attempts to spread the conflagrations of war, while they still create devastating suffering for large numbers of people, are being contained by the increasingly aware peace sentiments of the world's populations due in part to these populations' access to more accurate and more quickly-available information than has ever been the case before.

Re-evaluation Counseling has continued to spread. There are at least small groups of people engaged in systematic Co-Counseling activities in *eighty-one* countries at the present. An increasing number of Co-Counseling leaders are appearing at least semi-publicly as leaders of broad constituencies in the wide world.

Counseling theory and techniques continue to advance.

The List (a shorter title than was announced for it in *A Better World*) was published and is now about to appear in an expanded, revised, second edition that will be available to anyone who wishes to purchase it. Many pamphlets, increasingly by authors other than myself, are being issued in larger editions.

The promised book for eight- and nine-year-olds and my autobiography have not progressed rapidly. My improving health has seemed to lessen the urgency which I felt about them in 1992, and other publications have taken priority on my writing agenda.

My own re-emergence has progressed well. Now, in the middle of 1995, at the age of seventy-nine years, I am much more at peace with myself and have a broader perspective on my kind, friendly universe than I have ever had before.

—Harvey Jackins
1995

THE
KIND,
FRIENDLY
UNIVERSE

Accelerating
Into the Future

Are the Insights of Re-evaluation Counseling Decisive For the Future of the World?

Our universe began sometime between eight and eighteen billion years ago. Our solar system and our beautiful planet Earth have existed for about four billion years. The first forms of life evolved on Earth more than three billion years ago. Our species of human beings evolved to its present form about a hundred thousand years ago.

By that time our species had developed a large forebrain which gave us a great capacity for intelligent thinking. We also had developed the physical equipment for achieving detailed communication with each other through speech.

We retained, in common with all other forms of life, an inherent drive or "directive" to *survive,* to *reproduce,* and to *expand our numbers.*

EARLY RESTRAINTS ON OUR DOMINATION OF THE EARTH

We did not dominate our planet for most of our history. Our early struggles to survive included the resisting of attacks by the many micro-organisms which tend to affect us with disease and cause our deaths. We were treated as a source of food by some other large creatures and were subject to predation by them. We competed for food and habitat with a large number of other living forms. These factors, and the difficulty of preserving acquired knowledge from one generation to the next (before the invention of writing), had the effect of preventing us from over-crowding and over-dominating the earth for most of our species' existence. For much of our history, any unwise activities or carelessnesses on our part did not greatly affect the total environment around us.

POTENTIAL FOR MIS-USE OF OUR INCREASED ABILITIES

However, some warning signs of the potential hazards involved in misuse of our increased abilities appeared early. The development of efficient hunting tools *and* cooperation between *groups* of hunters seems to have led to the extermination or near-extermination of many other large mammals and birds. If we could treat them as food, or regard them as dangers, or view them as competitors for a habitat that we desired for ourselves, our species typically acted short-sightedly and self-centeredly in relation to the survival of other organisms.

PATTERNS OF GREED

With the invention of agriculture and animal husbandry the possibility of *organized societies* arose.

Patterns of greed and oppression were installed and then "justified" in these societies. It is understandable that in the presence of hunger, danger, and limited technology people would become anxious about their survival and the fulfillment of their needs. Under such conditions, patterns of compulsive greed would occasionally become installed by accidental circumstances. With the resulting *competition* between individuals, the "usefulness" of greed patterns as motivations and rules for living could seem attractive to the victors in such competitions, regardless of the misgivings of the vanquished or the questioning of these patterns by wiser individuals.

These patterns of greed, reinforced by repetition and "success," undoubtedly led to the exploitation of weaker or smaller individuals by stronger ones. This prepared the ground for rapidly-developing and rapidly-expanding slave-owner-slave societies.

These slaveowner-slave societies (and the other forms of oppressive societies, such as feudalism and capitalism, which followed) found mechanisms for the preservation and reproduction of themselves by installing *oppressions* of particular groups. These were groups such as the young, women, and members of so-called "races" which were labeled as "different" using any observable or imagined physical difference. All these particular oppressions divided the oppressed majority against each other and kept them submissive to the oppressive minority which ruled the society. *Institutions* would then arise, often taking the forms of *"religions"* and *"schools,"* for the deliberate installation of *patterns of being oppressed or being oppressors* (because these patterns led to the society "running well" from the viewpoint of the oppressors).

It is not farfetched to assume that these developments were rebelled against by many individuals. Thoughtful human observers probably questioned, expressed regret about, and resisted the wars, environmental destruction, genocide, and other greedy and wasteful behaviors. However, as long as there seemed to be unlimited planetary space to expand into, the greed-rewarding "success" of these short-sighted practices continued to dominate. The ruining of the environment in the eastern Mediterranean lands and the creation of deserts such as the Sahara must have caused great hardship to ordinary people. However, as long as new stretches of the planet lay open for occupation and exploitation, the results of these damaging activities did not lead the humans in the oppressive societies to insist on more rational social practices.

"GOOD OLD DAYS" NO BETTER

People in our generations who have tried to think outside the current social rigidities have often resorted to the viewpoint that times in the past were the "good old days," and that only in "modern" times have destructive practices on the part of humans created difficulties for ourselves. The supposition here is that in the past we humans were "noble savages," that we "used to" live in relative peace with each other and preserve the environment thoughtfully. Only in "modern" times, according to this supposition, have the bad tendencies of current populations come to play such a destructive, oppressive, and irrational role.

Modern research, however, has pretty well revealed that humans of the past behaved just as viciously in their times and in their generations as modern humans have.

A CONTINUING NEGATIVE APPEARANCE ON THE "BIG" QUESTIONS

Humans, with their presently accrued load of irrationality, systematically imposed and accumulated over six thousand years of existence in class societies, *do* continue to present an overwhelmingly negative picture on the "big" questions. These big questions include the social mistreatment of each other, the lack of care of the environment and of other species, and our failure to protect the future of the planet. It is understandable that modern researchers of our species' past tend to reach discouraging conclusions about the chances of wise, responsible behaviors being adopted by humans in the future.

KEY INSIGHTS ARE OFFERED BY RE-EVALUATION COUNSELING

We who have participated in developing Re-evaluation Counseling have important contributions to make on these questions. I think we also have the *responsibility* of making these contributions.

No other group of thinkers today realizes that humans actually function in two completely distinct modes, nor that these modes of functioning alternate in directing the behavior of individuals (and of the groups which are composed of the individuals).

Human intelligence is a continually flexible, continually-updating-itself mode of functioning. It continuously seeks additional information from the environment and from its own store of information accumulated from its own past experiences. Human intelligence integrates the information from both sources and as a result continuously modifies the conclusions it has reached in the past. Human intelligence functions towards a goal of *optimum outcome*, optimum survival for all factors in any situation which affect the person in any way. Human intelligence, when operating, always concludes that cooperation is more effective for survival than is competition. It keeps that conclusion as a background for all its more detailed evaluations.

Conditioned behavior, as distinct from and contrasted to the operations of human intelligence, is similar to the behavior of more primitive creatures. This mode of behavior operates on a stimulus-response basis. Creatures operating in this mode have *inherited* sets of stimulus-response patterns. They can change their inherited behavior during their lifetimes, however, by recording whatever goes on during any tense situation which they survive and substituting that recording for the instinctive patterns of response which they inherited. This acquired new behavior is likely to be somewhat more pro-survival than the inherited behavior.

Humans are vulnerable to *relapsing* to a similar kind of primitive functioning during any distressing situation. A recording of the distressing experience is then left upon them which contains the primitive stimulus-response type of behavior. When these recorded distress patterns are restimulated, the humans gripped by the patterns act on a stimulus-response basis. They become "addicted to" these behaviors in spite of the discomforts associated with them. Humans accumulate a great mass of such patterns when living within the operations of the oppressive societies.

Those of us who developed Re-evaluation Counseling were eventually able to notice that certain "built-in" processes of recovery from such rigid patterns existed and tended to operate spontaneously in safe, positive situations (especially if the person was listened to and paid attention to by another intelligence). These abilities to recover were observed to operate through a series of processes that we have characterized with the name of "discharge." These are manifested by the shedding of tears; by trembling, shaking, and perspiring; by laughter with cold skin temperature; by angry "storming"; by laughter with warm skin temperature; by non-repetitive talk; and by yawning.

OUR *BASIC* NATURE AS HUMANS IS INTELLIGENT, COOPERATIVE, BENIGN

The results of observing and encouraging these processes with many people over a long period of time made it possible for us to conclude that the flexible intelligent behavior inherent to humans is restored to the person after enough discharge. Over time we came to the conclusion that this intelligent behavior is actually the *basic* nature of our species. We came to realize that the observed relapses to a more primitive, rigid, unintelligent type of behavior are temporary suspensions of our inherent functioning. These suspensions, over a period of time, have occluded and masked our real nature.

This conclusion, that the real nature of human beings is totally intelligent, benign, cooperative, and caring, opens a completely new, dependable vista of the future of humankind. We can observe that there is an overall upward trend in the universe of which we are a part and within which we play a leading role. For the universe as a whole, for the world of life, and for the human race, thrilling, limitless future prospects open up. If people know what we know, if they have this background knowledge, they will necessarily reach optimistic and encouraging conclusions about our future.

OUR CRUCIAL ROLE AS RCers

Only a few hundred thousand people have so far been exposed to and grasped this picture and have moved to put it to use in their own lives and in their interaction with the world.

As yet only a small group of us has grasped the fundamental reality of our evolutionary turning-the-corner-toward-intelligence. This has revealed a different picture of our humanness. This new view makes it plain that *intelligence* is really our *basic* operating nature. Only a small group of us as yet understands that the actual enormous intelligence of all humans has been obscured in the way it has until now by the phenomenon of *acquired distress patterns*.

Only a few of us as yet know that these distress patterns can be largely prevented by carefully planned environments for humans when they are young, by trying to avoid hurtful experiences occurring to children, and by providing the opportunity for thorough discharge in the few cases where distresses happen in spite of our care.

Only a few of us as yet know confidently that distress patterns, once installed, can be removed by simple procedures. Only a small group of us as yet know how to use these simple procedures and are experienced in using them with a significant number of people. (It has only been forty-five years since these procedures were first noticed and correctly interpreted.)

This places those of us who have been exposed to, who have grasped, and who have accepted this knowledge in a crucial position.

If a good future for the world of life and for the human race depends on this knowledge being communicated and used by a decisive section of the five and a half billion humans presently on our planet (and I think this is exactly true) then an engaging and thrilling perspective beckons us into our futures.

We who know Re-evaluation Counseling well not only *know how to*, we not only *can*, but in a sense we almost *must* lead extremely purposeful lives. We *must* play a decisive role, *must* assume lives of great meaning, *must* tackle the biggest job and the most influential roles that humans have ever been called on to tackle and play. We *must* live lives of loving closeness to other humans. We are almost compelled to live lives of intense satisfaction, becoming the most effective "do-gooders" in the history of our species.

There is greater *informed unity* between *a much wider variety of people* in the Re-evaluation Counseling Communities at present than has heretofore been seen on our planet. The Re-evaluation Counseling Community and its intricate relationships have survived long enough and have resisted enough kinds of attacks already as to leave the impression that the Community and its content are *invulnerable.*

We have moved slowly but well. We are furnishing the world the needed knowledge of the essential goodness of intelligent human beings. This is giving, and will give, heart and power to all the world's peoples. The people's responses to this knowledge will eventually free all of us from the oppressive conditioning and the oppressive social institutions in ways whose descriptions are the principal content of this book. The disasters which we have feared will not take place.

New Frontiers in Our Thinking

Re-evaluation Counseling consists of a set of ideas, a set of loosely organized relationships between people in eighty countries of the world (so far), and activities to further these ideas and these relationships and to bring about their increasing effectiveness in the world and the universe.

From time to time developments and "corner-turnings" in our thinking create *new* frontiers in this set of ideas, frontiers which need to be explored, understood, developed, and practiced. Some of these frontiers recently opened or needing to be opened at this time (January, 1995), are the following:

• **The extension of "Inclusion" to every human on our planet, with no exceptions.** (Every living human is to be assumed to be fully and adequately human in every way, treated as such, and given full respect, support, encouragement, and adequate use of all available resources.)

• **The extension of "Cherishing" to every form of life on our planet.** Each form of life is assumed to be of priceless value because of the unique complexity it has achieved as well as its possible utility to us and its beauty to our beholding. (Means of protection against forms of life dangerous to us may and should be devised, but our goal shall be the

Appeared in **Present Time** No. 98, January 1995.

preservation of all existing species of living things and *re-constitution* through our increasing genetic engineering knowledge of any species previously extinguished.)

• **The extension of "Caretaking" to every factor in our total environment.** (All pollution and degradation of the atmosphere, waters, and soils of our planet are to be terminated and reversed. The environment shall be restored to approximate the natural balance it possessed before the overcrowding and over-exploitation by our species, before the distress patterns which were imposed upon our species had contaminated it and interfered with it. The environment shall then be allowed to develop with a minimum of interference from our operations.)

• **The elimination from among us of the nearly-universal chronic patterns of** *feeling and believing that we are unloved.* (Counseling in the direction indicated by the leading-edge technique of asking repeatedly, "Why do you love me, counselor?")

• **The elimination of the nearly-universal and deeply-installed patterns of** *separation* **of all humans from each other.** (Counseling in the direction indicated by the leading-edge technique of using the phrase, "You and me, Jane [John], completely close, forever," followed after each repetition by a statement of the client's *first thought.*)

• **The elimination from among us of the nearly-universal** *overall timidity,* completely foreign to our inherent natures but patterned upon us by a lifetime of conditioning begun in our earliest moments of life. (Counseling in the direction of assuming complete power to achieve or bring about anything we rationally desire. [Kipling: "If you can meet with Triumph or Disaster and treat those two impostors just the same."])

• Achieving an operating relationship between all of us based on the *reality* that each one of us is *completely* good, *completely* intelligent, *completely* able, *completely* powerful, and *completely* capable of *acting on all this in all circumstances.* (Counseling in the direction of agreeing to the complete distinction between actual reality and "pseudo-reality," and agreeing to examine all situations and answer all questions only from the viewpoint of *actual reality,* then carrying out these agreements.)

• Achieving a universal agreement among us that persistently offering and publicizing rational solutions to problems (individual and social) will always eventually win majority, and later, universal support. (Persisting in offering rational solutions to any problem no matter how repeatedly the solution is rejected. Alternative irrational, oppressive solutions will always fail. The opposition to rational solutions is certain to eventually be worn out.)

• Accepting the reality of the universal attractiveness and charisma of every human who commits himself or herself to a rational outlook on life and to functioning rationally. (Include *yourself* as such a human.) (Everyone yearns to find a person that is safe to admire and to love. By your thinking and actions, give people reason to decide you are safe in this way. Allow people to love you, support you, and follow you.)

• Accepting the necessity and correctness of women RCers taking responsibility for solving and overcoming any difficulties which until now have delayed the development of a powerful RC Men's Liberation Movement and an *effective cadre of men's leaders.* (Failure to do this until now is simply one aspect of persisting patterns of women's powerlessness. Women already see clearly the patterns in which men RCers are "stuck," and they discuss them with each other continuously. They need to share this information with men clearly and forcefully, help devise effective contradictions to the men's patterns, and *require and assist* men to move to discharge these patterns.)

• **Facing clearly and awarely that all class societies to date, including the present one, have sanctified GREED as the *highest priority motivation* for *all* people *in all situations*, and that this 6,000 years of conditioning must be exposed and repudiated in all fields of life.** (Planning and beginning a campaign to secure a universal attitude in our societies of rejecting greed as an acceptable motivation for anything.)

• **Realizing that *competition*, in the sense that that word is used in our cultures, is *an inhuman activity*. *Cooperation* is the effective way of functioning for our basic human nature. *Competition* is an invention of the oppressive, class society.** (Enhancing and praising every tendency to cooperation visible in human functioning, in various cultures, and in religious and poetic traditions. Decrying, exposing, opposing, and eliminating every expression of competition, including the most presently "sanctified" examples in the present cultures and societies.)

• **Universally accepting and practicing the viewpoint that *all individuals are delightfully unique* but that *differences* between individuals are trivial, shallow, and unimportant, and that commonalities between all individuals are deep, powerful, and important.** (In particular, members of all classes are oppressed by and are the victims of classism. The class society is equally the enemy of, the damager of, and the oppressor of owning-class people, "middle-class" people, and working-class people, and all have a common interest in eliminating classism.)

Another Step Toward
More Skillful Counseling

Co-Counseling has worked well and continues to improve in effectiveness for a growing number of people. Part of its improved effectiveness is certainly because of the gains which the people acting as counselors have previously made when they were *clients*. Part of the gains also are surely because successive breakthroughs in clarifying our theory have allowed us to be more accurate about our role as counselors.

In the last two years, after realizing the central importance of the concept of "contradiction," we have been able to relate all of the successful past approaches ("techniques") of counseling to a general framework. All of our past successful approaches to counseling can be seen as some form or other of applying the "contradiction principle" in a session. By *contradiction* we mean anything that allows the victim or bearer of the pattern to realize that the pattern is NOT present time reality. When a distress pattern is thus "contradicted," and the contradiction is persisted in, the pattern becomes converted to discharge.

The "exchange of roles" by the client and the counselor has been described in *Present Time* in the past. It is a remarkably

Appeared in **Present Time** No. 92, July 1993.

effective application of "contradiction" in a way that often converts patterns that have previously resisted counseling to easy discharge.

The "repeated question" approach, ("Why do you love me, counselor?"), was developed soon after the exchange-of-roles breakthrough, and provided a clear-cut example of the effectiveness of the client avoiding *any* "rehearsal" of the distress.

A NEW APPROACH

A new approach, about three weeks old at the time that I first write this article, seems to make it possible to have the time spent in session be totally contradictory to the client's distress pattern and completely lacking in any "rehearsal" of it. Below is a possible scenario of such a session:

Counselor: **Will you try a new approach that I have found to be effective?**

Client: **What is it?**

Counselor: **I am assuming here that you and I are in agreement that the *actual reality* of the universe, the way things really are, is different than and distinct from the *pseudo-reality* interpretation of the universe which has been presented to us by oppression, by other people's patterns, by misinformation, and by the societies in which we live. This includes the false picture which our own remaining patterns often try to impose on us as a substitute for actual reality. I am assuming that you and I agree that the actual reality is completely distinct from this pseudo-reality.**

Client: **I agree to that.**

Counselor: I also assume that we agree to a similar distinction between your own real nature and the false pictures of your nature which patterns, oppression, false information, and any remaining distresses tend to offer.

Client: *(perhaps after a pause)* I agree to that.

Counselor: I'm going to ask you some very simple questions. I want your agreement in advance that you will answer these simple questions only from the position of the actual reality of the universe and of yourself, not from any of the pseudo-reality which may come to your mind. Do not express any pseudo-reality. Do not describe any of your patterns, even if you are pulled by the patterns' claims to be "interesting," or "needed to give the whole picture," or "needed to be expressed in order to be rejected." I will remind you and interrupt you if necessary, but I will count on you staying committed to answering from actual reality. I will count on you being willing to give the same answer many, many times as you try to get in touch with the reality of it.

Client: Okay, I'm committed.

Counselor: Okay, thank you, esteemed and excellent client. *(In a warm, encouraging, affectionate voice)*: "How *good* are you?"

Client: *(usually discharges one way or other)*

(With some clients discharge is immediate and voluminous. Other clients seem to have to think intently before the contradiction that produces the discharge begins to operate, begins to "sink in." Sometimes the client forgets the commitment and begins to "explain" instead of answering the question. The counselor can then remind the client to "just answer the question.")

The counselor's job is to wait—relaxed, calm, pleased, and confident. If the client seems to be losing touch with the expectation that the question be answered, the counselor may repeat the question.

Client: (may say) **Oh, I'm pretty good.**

Counselor: (in response to the client) **That would certainly be true from my observation, but "pretty" might seem to be making comparisons with others. Do you feel able to tell me that you are "*completely* good"?**

The client is usually discharging by this time, sometimes loudly, sometimes quietly. The discharge may be laughter, tears, shaking, angry words, or yawns. As the discharge proceeds the client may drop his or her eyes away from the counselor's friendly gaze, may seem to slowly lose touch with the concept of his or her own goodness. The client may stop discharging and begin to look "shut-down" or "confused." If the counselor continues to look warmly at the client and keeps his or her attention on the "goodness" of the client, the client's gaze will eventually return to meet the counselor's gaze. From the appearances, it seems that the client suddenly again remembers the concept of his or her own complete goodness. Apparently the distresses which had begun to cluster around this concept are now once again contradicted, and the client resumes discharge.

If the client does not discharge steadily or voluminously, the difficulty is probably that the client is not making direct enough contact with the concept of the goodness of himself or herself. The client can be assisted to do this by the counselor asking the client to say, "I am completely good," in a warm, proud, pleased-with-himself-or-herself tone. (The counselor's tone being warm and pleased with the client will also make a difference.) Even so, it may sometimes take considerable time for the reality to "sink in." If the client is encouraged to repeat the phrase, "I am completely good" to the counselor, and the counselor agrees, the client soon will make close enough contact with the reality of his or her "goodness" that the discharge will begin to be ongoing.

I have not yet, as counselor (at this time of writing), stayed with the use of the answer to any single question for more than about two hours. I have, however, gotten a clear impression that we could stay with any one question for a large number of hours or for a large number of sessions, with profound and excellent results.

The fact that there is no time or effort spent by the client-counselor pair in expressing, going over, or "rehearsing" the distress but only in contradicting and discharging the distress, is probably the reason that this appears to be one of the most effective modes of counseling that we have ever used.

The profundity of realizing that one is *completely* good, and the efficiency of the conversion to discharge of any distress that would try to oppose that realization, is very impressive and satisfying. Many distresses that previously have seemed to be quite intransigent melt easily (if, sometimes, slowly). There is no "restimulation" or residue of upset after the session because the client's attention has been wholly on reality all the time.

To date, I have worked with approximately thirty clients this way. So far I have always started out with the question, "How *good* are you?" I have usually followed up a period with that question with other questions. Some of the questions I have used are: "How *innocent* are you?" "How *pure* are

you?" "How *confident* are you?" "How *intelligent* are you?"
"How *powerful* are you?" "How *free* are you?" "How free are
you to plan your life just exactly the way you wish it to go?"
"How competent are you to see to it that your life takes place
just the way you want it to take place, after you have planned
it?" "How able are you to see that another person, such as
your Co-Counselor, attains everything in his or her life that
he or she desires?" "How neat, efficient, and well-organized
are you?" "How rigorous are you in examining and noting
any non-survival practices which have become attached to
your life, and how rigorous and self-initiating are you in
eliminating them?"

All of these questions need to eventually be answered with
sentences that mean, "I am completely innocent, intelligent,
etc." Each such answer needs to be persisted with as long as
the time permits. The process is very satisfying to both the
client and the counselor.

I have hopes that this is the beginning of a profound
change in counseling sessions. It has the possibility of eliminating *in practice* the spending of time and attention in
sessions in description of, rehearsal of, and dramatizations of
distress. I am hopeful that mastering this approach can
substantially expedite the *wholesale* contradiction of, and
discharge of, and re-emergence from the distresses which, up
until now, have afflicted our lives so persistently.

Mechanical repetition of the phrases such as, "I am completely good," will not suffice to bring these exciting results,
although it may tend to move the client in that direction by
the client's beginning to think about the words that he or she
has been saying so mechanically. It may be that the high level
of success with this approach so far is due, in part, to the fact
that I have worked mostly with leaders of the Community
and so have incidentally "sorted out" people who are pre-

pared by their previous work and gains to really make and keep a commitment to participate in the session only from the standpoint of the actual reality of themselves and the universe around them.

I think the promising aspects of the results so far are because we have here come upon a way in which most clients can make a keepable commitment to deny attention to their distresses, and to repeatedly dwell on and express fundamental contradictions to those distresses. I think that this gives us access to the tremendous ability of the client's mind to discharge, re-evaluate, and think when it is not hobbled by rehearsing the distresses which have claimed part of its attention in most past sessions.

The "Reality Agreement" Approach to a Session

The term "reality agreement" was decided upon as a name for this approach or "technique" after the article about it was written for the July *Present Time*. Many people have been discussing its use (as the news about it has spread by grapevine and telephone and workshop), and many names were being used for it. So it was decided to settle on "Reality Agreement" as a common title to use with each other when we discuss our experiences.

I will relate some further experiences of mine in using it, give some reports that I have heard, and, at the end of this article, reprint comments from some letters I have received.

It is a common conclusion by the people who've been using this that the basic reason for the effectiveness of the procedure is the *agreement* between the client and the counselor that they will communicate, answer questions, and support each other within their commitment to *deal only with the rational side* of the universe, persons, or situations. The two formally agree that the irrational, patterned, *pseudo-reality* will not be allowed to intrude into their communication or their attentions, and, if it does intrude, it will be rejected and attention returned to actual reality.

Appeared in **Present Time** No. 93, October 1993.

Reports from some Co-Counselors tell of trying to simply repeat the questions that they had seen work well in a demonstration (in which the agreement had been made) but not themselves making the agreement. They were disappointed. Without the agreement, the technique either "didn't work" or seemed to "run out" very quickly.

Other reports say, and my own experience agrees with them, that when the agreement has been made and understood by the client, the counselor often seems to have little more to do than to "be there." The counselor pays attention and is present as a *reminder* of the agreement. The client moves from one thought to another spontaneously and with continuing discharge, gaining momentum as time goes on. The client often reports feeling a sense of elation, discovery, and liberation which, as it is communicated briefly to the counselor, leads to fresh bursts of discharge.

The following is one version of the way the crucial *agreement* can be set up:

Counselor: For this to work, it is important that you and I are in agreement that the *actual reality* of the universe and everything in it is completely distinct from the *pseudo-reality* which has been accumulated from patterns, oppression, misinformation, lack of information, and mistakes of the past, which has often been presented to us in the past as a substitute for reality. Are we agreed that these two things, the reality and the pseudo-reality, are completely distinct and do not have anything in common at all?

Client (sometimes immediately, sometimes after taking thought): Yes, I agree that this is so.

Counselor: And in particular, the sub-set of reality which is *you, the actual nature of yourself,* is different than the

24

pseudo-reality which has often been pushed on you as a description of yourself: the invalidations, misunderstandings, disappointments, and oppressions which you have been "told" are what you are like.

Client: Yes, I agree that they are completely different.

Counselor: With that agreement between us, I'm going to ask you some very simple questions, and I need your agreement that you will answer them only from the viewpoint of reality itself, without any pseudo-reality being allowed into your answers. You may find this difficult (some people do), but if you slip, I will remind you to keep your answers based in reality, standing firmly on that viewpoint and not allowing any pseudo-reality into your answers.

Client: Yes, I agree to that.

Counselor: How *good* are you?

Client: Oh, pretty good. In fact, I could say very good. Sticking to reality only, I am *completely* good. (Client begins to discharge.)

To start with "How *good* are you?" has generally been profoundly effective, apparently because the client's private knowledge that he or she is "completely good" contradicts the widespread invalidation which all of us have endured in our lives. When things are "right" between the particular counselor and the particular client, hours of discharge are available without much further activity from the counselor except his or her reassuring, committed presence.

My own experiences are leading me to think that the less of an active role I play, once the process has begun well for the client, the more skillfully the client will develop the ability for himself or herself of silently seeking out and examining a long series of past conflicts with the confidence of this new viewpoint. The discharge process will tend to gain momentum as it proceeds.

For many people, at least, the calm, silent expectation of the counselor that the client will proceed mentally to review present and past reality from the viewpoint of his or her "goodness," "innocence," "purity," etc., etc., etc. is more helpful than any intervention from the counselor. I have found that some of my own distresses (anxiety, over-eagerness) push me to tend to "help" too much. If I can remember to not "help," or if I restrict any interventions by me to saying, "Stay with it," the independence and initiative of the client gather strength and momentum. If the client is having trouble keeping attention on the answers to the question, the counselor can simply repeat the question softly and confidently.

It is true that many experienced clients will be found to have been "trained" to expect the counselor's intervention (and stop and wait for it), but the "training" can be undone by the counselor waiting longer and longer intervals between interventions, while appearing relaxed and confident to any questioning looks which the client turns on him or her.

We began working with this approach with the exploration of goodness, innocence, purity, confidence, competence, intelligence, and power. It seems as if we can probably move effectively also into the areas of affection, closeness, love, commitment, responsibility, and "ability to be self-starting."

There has been some experimentation taking into account the observed nature of particular chronic difficulties that the particular client has endured. When the client is able to respond cooperatively, these experiments have been effective. Among some of these questions that have worked well are: "How attractive are you?" "How charming are you?" "How successful are you?" "How much do I love you?"

I speculate that we may here be uncovering the tracks of a very ancient human mistake. If this is true, this mistake has side-tracked and distorted human progress for a long period of time.

Other species of humans besides our own have lived in the past. We are sure of their existence from the evidence of fossil remains. All present humans, however, are members of one very closely related sub-species that is estimated to have been in existence for approximately one hundred thousand years.

If the earliest members of our sub-species were as much like ourselves as the available evidence indicates, they certainly were vulnerable to being hurt physically and emotionally. This means they were vulnerable to acquiring patterns, by accident or by contagion, even though the principal current mechanism for installing patterns—oppression—was still a long way in the future.

Once a distress pattern was installed upon them, these forebears of ours must have noticed, perhaps from introspection, that part of themselves (their humanness and their intelligence) was not working as well as it had before the hurtful experience. They undoubtedly tried to do something about it.

If they responded in the way in which they had learned to deal with other difficulties in their lives, they undoubtedly tried to "take a look at" the phenomenon, "think about it," and "find a solution." It seems probable that this is just what our forebears did. For them and for us, when we have an

*objective problem outside of ourselves to be dealt with, the
more attention we pay to it, the more we think about it, the
more likely we are to find a solution.*

*Unfortunately, as I think we are finally coming to clearly
understand,* putting attention on a problem caused by a
pattern *only helps in very special circumstances, that is,
when someone else will pay attention to us, when discharge
is permitted and encouraged, and when some motivation to
persist in the process is furnished.* To pay attention to a
problem caused by a pattern in usual circumstances *is to
become victimized by the pattern, to have it extend its sway
over us, to add another layer of distress to the pattern for
each time we try to deal with it in this way. Dealing well
with a problem caused by a pattern involves* not *putting
one's thoughtful attention on it, involves placing one's attention* away *from the distress and on information that*
contradicts *the distress, involves taking an attitude that
refuses to identify the pattern with oneself.*

*We have, in the last forty years, made many partial
attempts in this direction. We have talked of and used
"pleasant memories," "the benign reality," "the upward
trend," "reclaiming power," and many other concepts point-
ing in this direction. We have increasingly noticed and
proposed the effectiveness of "contradiction." We have
cheered the emergence of the "repeated question" technique
("Why do you love me, counselor?") as involving* no *rehearsal of the distress.*

I hope, expect, and am somewhat confident that these
present developments around the Reality Agreement approach may mark a decisive turning point in our progress. If
we can master the use of these insights, it should be possible
to proceed directly to the elimination of the great piles of

distresses (invalidation, self-doubt, fearful conformity, and submission) that have visibly accumulated upon almost every human.

It may be possible to regain the zest, confidence, initiative, and power that can change the functioning of the world decisively and in a very short time.

> The article "Another Step Toward More Skillful Counseling" is brilliant and has helped. I'm working in my sessions on "How competent am I to see to it that my life takes place just the way I want it to take place after I have planned it?" I'm also starting to work on "How able am I to see to it that my Co-Counselors attain everything in their lives that they desire?"
>
> Esther Jackson
> Albany, New York, USA

I've been using the "Reality Agreement Approach" for myself and lots of other people. For the most part, it goes well. I certainly notice, for myself, the corner I am turning in terms of keeping my attention on reality. Sometimes I find myself slipping into repetitive, wooden ways of saying a phrase. In general, it has been helpful to reconstruct the entire argument as to why I am completely good or why I have reason to be supremely confident or how the universe is completely delighted with my presence. Whatever distress pulls at me, before long I am contradicting it from this perspective.

I have found that some less experienced clients virtually give up on the agreement to answer from reality. In one case I went back with the client to the very concept of a reality that is not patterned and had to get her agreement to assume that reality (as we use the word in RC) *exists* and is not just a theory. We couldn't get a solid contradiction to the early hurts that still made the client feel limited without the assumption that a non-patterned reality exists.

Jenny Helbraun
San Francisco, California, USA

The "new technique," the idea of answering questions from the point of view of reality only, works very powerfully. It seems that this and many other new "techniques" are all ways of helping to get people to put their attention off of their distress, that the key insight here is the idea of counseling with attention away from distress.

Phillip Bennett
Ithaca, New York, USA

The Reality Agreement technique works like magic here, too. No bad sessions, no disappointments, good discharge, and an enormous release of new, good energy; realism, and zest.

Eric Fokke
Amsterdam, The Netherlands

I have had the opportunity to work with Harvey a few times on making the distinction between pseudo-reality and reality, and agreeing to only talk about what is real in session. I have also worked with about fifty people in this way with great success. Upon reflection, I think this newest method is a theoretical advance in assisting the client to initiate and take complete responsibility for the client's own re-emergence. We have a long history of successful understandings in this area, and this newest method provides the best contradiction to date.

Charles Esser
Philadelphia, Pennsylvania, USA

My work with the reality agreement continues to be profound. This work is quite different from taking directions and trying to reach for them. To be honest, "positive directions" never worked well for me.

I use the reality agreement completely differently. It forces me to decide the truth of the situation and then, when I'm able to answer the question, I can say the phrase out loud because I see it is the truth. When I get asked a particular question, my mind goes right to the place where I can't decide, don't know, or where the moment of internalized oppression was set in and I lost that particular knowledge about myself. I then hang right there in that place of not knowing and then use the opportunity to really decide what must be true. Unlike positive directions, I use the reality agreement as a wedge to force my brain completely out of any distress.

Where I have seen the agreement not work well, it appeared to me that the client was still in the position of not believing the phrase and then using it to try to bring about her agreement. At the Continental Conference, I saw this old approach once. You held out the reality agreement like a positive direction, and the client got to rehearse all the funny little ways she wanted to whittle it down or rehearse her distress. This seems to me like the old approach of the client trying to use a direction to dig her way out of her distress. Instead, I prefer to climb to the top of the pile of my distress, survey the whole scene, and pronounce its untruth. I'd be interested to know if this difference in understanding and use of the agreement is unique to me or would have more broad use by others. At any rate, this has reliable and profound results for me, and I continue to use it in almost all of my sessions. The only sessions where I don't use it are when I need to process and review many decisions and events of an overwhelming day/week, and yawn and yawn and yawn.

Judy Kay
Tacoma, Washington, USA

The agreement to answer from reality is the best way of 'keeping my attention off distress' that I've ever had. It extends completely out of session. I think the agreement and the logic is very powerful. Just as we realized, ten years ago or so, that we had made an agreement to be counselor which we then broke, and that helped tremendously in getting us back on track, the agreement to answer from the truth, from the real, the benign reality, cannot be just left in session. It's powerful, pervasive, and I like it.

Isabel Auerbach
San Francisco, California, USA

Sybil Moses came back and shared the latest insights and counselling techniques which are now spreading fast through our South Antrim and Belfast RC Community. How powerful am I? ... Completely!!!

Sue Holden
Craigavon, County Armagh, Northern Ireland

THE WORD FROM AROUND ISRAEL IS THAT THE "REALITY AGREEMENT" IS WORKING FANTASTICALLY WELL.

Sara Kallai
Jerusalem, Israel

Seeing the "reality agreement" used to great effect by Russ Vernon-Jones at his recent workshop helped me understand the technique better. (Some approaches to counseling leap easily from the pages of **Present Time** *into practice; for others, I need to see it to know how to begin to do it.) It's a powerful approach when applied thoughtfully. I've often wondered how you keep coming up with new counseling techniques. Do they emerge in practice, or do you sit down with a problem and devise a solution and then test it?*

Sue Haring
Brooklyn, New York, USA

I used the reality agreement with tremendous success in my men's support group this week. Everyone got the idea. It is basically a pure contradiction. It is very empowering for the client to decide to answer from the viewpoint of reality. We actually had our best success with the question "How safe are you?"

John Kinsella
San Francisco,
California, USA

The Black Liberation workshops are done. We continued the work with the "reality agreement" and people seemed to move quite profoundly. Thanks for how well you continue to think about us.

Barbara Love
Amherst, Massachusetts, USA

I thought the work on the reality agreement broke important new ground. I was moved by your candidness and the way you and Tim cooperated in leading. Since returning home I've used the reality agreement to good effect. It certainly puts a check on the useless dramatizing.

Ellie Marsh
Albany, New York, USA

The workshop was great. It was good to watch your funny and easy leadership. The best theory for me was to hear about the reality and pseudo-reality and making every day new decisions to stay with the actual reality.

Susanne Köhr
Havixbeck, Germany

I would like to report the results of some sessions using the 'actual reality' approach.

Lin Parker shared her experiences from the working-class conference in New Jersey today. She used her information about the nature of men's oppression and the nature of women's oppression to tweak the contradiction by asking men ,"How proud are you?" and by asking the women, "How much in charge are you?", after summarizing the nature of reality and pseudo-reality and concluding agreements with her clients.

These demonstrations were kept quite short, but by thinking about each person well, she showed how effective it is to enlist the client to lead and how productive it is to frame the questions around what you know and can observe about your client.

Larry Gardiner
Liverpool, England

I am *very* pleased with the reality agreement work. Thanks so much for putting it forward this way. Somehow this just seems to be the right thing for getting the client's intelligence to work on his/her own behalf in the discharge process—and what a powerful lever that intelligence is!

Pamela Haines
Philadelphia,
Pennsylvania, USA

The reality agreement is a brilliant new understanding of the basic concept of complete self-appreciation (at the very least). Right now the most useful question for me is "how adequate are you?" The answer is, "I am completely adequate." This may not seem like it fits the bill, but since a significant part of my chronic distress sounds like this: "I'm supposed to be exceptional, and I am a miserable failure," it works like a charm.

Amy Kietzman
Philadelphia, Pennsylvania, USA

I just led a wonderful owning-class-support-group leaders' workshop in my house. There were twenty-four of us packed in tightly.

It was extremely good fun, as well as a thoughtful, safe, place with a lot of good work done on the reality agreement. I'd never seen it demonstrated before. It is *really* good news. Thank you for thinking it up—it'll save new RCers a lot of time! (And hopefully us oldies too.)

Hilary Plews
London, England

I am excited about using the reality agreement as counselor, leader, and client. It seems to be just what we need. It looks to me like a specific way to fully involve the client on the side of what good counselors have already been doing.... You talked in this direction a couple of years ago when you spoke of "organizing the client."

John Schmieding
Athens, Ohio, USA

I am sure you are hearing this generally: the reality agreement is catching on like a brush fire. Apparently this is precisely what many of us have been needing, "packaged" just right. I hope you are as pleased as you have a right to be.

Ellen Deacon
Philadelphia, Pennsylvania, USA

At my teachers' and leaders' class I did some good demonstrations of the Reality Agreement technique. People loved it. I also did it in my fundamentals class, my people-of-color class, and with all of my counselors, and it worked well in every instance. It's been a lot of fun coming up with questions that really target each person's chronic. I've been doing well with it also; as soon as I catch myself rehearsing my distress (which I can do a lot) I immediately ask my counselor to start the agreement, and between the two of us we come up with a question that will contradict the distress I was trying to discharge. It has worked like a dream. Lynn Sahaj and I have been doing that with each other a lot.

Dvora Slavin
Oak Park, Maryland, USA

THE CONFERENCE WAS WONDERFUL. THE GROWTH IN THE COMMUNITIES WAS OBVIOUS TO ME. WE HAVE COME A LONG WAY! THE COUNSELING I DID USING THE REALITY APPROACH WAS EFFECTIVE IN MANY WAYS. I THINK THE APPROACH HAS PROFOUND IMPLICATIONS FOR OUR WORK AND FOR SOCIETAL TRANSFORMATION. I ENCOURAGE YOU TO KEEP EXPLORING IT AND WRITING ABOUT IT.

Julian Weissglass
Santa Barbara, California, USA

There's another way your "new approach" can work! I stumbled on it by accident.

In last Tuesday's class, my teacher introduced your new approach and invited us to try it for our sessions in group time. I wanted to, but I had just that day received a letter from Peter Cross, telling me that his wife had died. Do you remember putting us in touch with each other way back in '91? We have been writing ever since, and Peter's letters shine with goodness.

I spent fifteen minutes telling of their long struggles with her Alzheimer's disease, and of how well he had used the RC process. Tears ran down my face as I recalled Peter's loyalty, faithfulness, integrity, and love. Faced with one of the most challenging, long-term situations I could imagine, Peter had been victorious. He had kept thinking: he had made things right for her; he had made things right for himself.

I didn't realize until the next morning that what I was discharging was hopelessness. *It is possible to get it right!* I hadn't been aware of carrying hopelessness—but later that night, almost without effort, I boldly made something right for myself, something I'd been wanting to improve for a long time.

So I had used your new approach after all. I had kept my attention on the actual reality of Peter's goodness. One person staying out of his distress had given me something to focus on besides mine. We can do that for each other!

Could it be that we aren't limited to identifying and contradicting our distress—we could hold our attention on the goodness and beauty of the universe, and the hopelessness would roll off? It would be like self-appreciation, but of the whole universe's Self of which we are a part. I think I shall try a session on "Reality is Benign."

Jane Heald
Swarthmore, Pennsylvania, USA

Can We Eliminate the Patterns
Which Have Been Inhibiting
Our Initiatives and Our Courage?

Some of the articles in this issue of *Present Time* are written by people who are telling of their first contacts with RC ideas. They are often very impressed with what a difference this contact has made in their functioning and in their attitudes towards life. Most of us current readers of *Present Time* have experienced this effect of "first knowledge" about the "RC viewpoint." It is sometimes good to recall this.

Some of these early insights were: finding that we *can do something* about the factors that are degrading our living; realizing that we are not helpless pawns to an imposed inevitability; glimpsing that behind every antagonist's pattern is a human who would prefer to be our ally; beginning to realize that there is nothing "wrong" with anybody except the results of their having been mistreated. All these insights have made a great difference to the way we live in the world, to our perception of our lives.

This is true about what we have grasped in the past, what we have already integrated into our thinking. Our as-yet-undischarged patterns, however, we have tended to still view as "inevitable," to assume that they are too difficult to

Appeared in **Present Time** No. 95, April 1994.

challenge or change. We have tended to still think that we are "pawns of fate" in relation to the larger affairs of our lives. We have "taken for granted" such factors as the terrible functioning of the economy and the growing unemployment and have tended to accept the roles assigned to us by the society because of our economic classes, our "races," or our genders.

At RC leadership conferences proposals have usually been made to challenge such submissive acceptances. Good programs have been adopted and circulated within the Community. However, the organizational steps for carrying out the best proposals and policies have often been shunted to one side. The leadership and leadership structure have sometimes become preoccupied with routine activity or, worse yet, have allowed negative criticisms and personal attacks to divert the attention of the Communities.

We have certainly been paying at least lip-service to these good proposals. What has been missing has often been taking initiative to actually carry them out determinedly. In the past we have not always resisted a patterned pull to become distracted and postpone crucial iniatives while we dealt with more routine challenges.

This might have seemed acceptable from the viewpoint of middle-class confusion. However, we have responsibility for all the members of the human race. We cannot postpone that responsibility. This is damaging to the world as a whole. It also blights any one of us who subsides into such submission to the oppressive culture's patterns.

Our planet at present contains millions of species of living things. Every part of this rich treasure is valuable beyond calculation. Such richness has only been attained by the intense evolutionary activity of life acting through eons of time. We cannot afford to just wring our hands and act powerless about the current rapid extinction of so many forms of life. Unless we act decisively, we will have missed a priceless opportunity. It is time for us to boldly and effectively demand that the whole society put the health of the environment and the preservation of all existing species of living things ahead of profit, *ahead* of "national" goals.

It is time to interrupt overpopulation patterns anywhere in the world. The populations which up to now are still increasing will cease doing so (with great relief) given a minimum of assistance from modern science and a world program of guaranteed employment and health care.

It is time for many of us to invade the presently-operating corrupt and deceitful political processes and turn them into an arena of struggle for a world in which profits are not allowed to take precedence over human needs.

Why have humans so often relapsed into powerlessness and defeatism in the past? Why have we humans tended to settle for distraction and routine? It *has to be* the effect of chronic patterns which the oppressive society has installed upon us earlier.

Can we contradict these patterns? Can we systematically eliminate them? Can we force them to discharge by *acting* on our theoretical knowledge of our real nature and our power? Can we accelerate this discharge by taking such action?

I ask you who are reading this: do you agree with me that the actual reality of the universe is completely different than the "pseudo-reality" which has been pushed at us as a substitute (a pseudo-reality which has been composed of misinformation, oppression, internalized oppression, pat-

terns, and confusion)? If you agree that reality and this "pseudo-reality" have nothing in common, I then ask you: do you agree that the portion of actual reality which is *you,* yourself, is completely different than the "pseudo-reality" picture of yourself? (This pseudo-reality is made up of the criticisms, invalidations, condemnations, and belittling that society and its institutions have tried to make you think is the real you.) If you agree with me that these two characterizations of yourself are completely different, then, on the basis of that agreement, I will ask you some questions. I ask your agreement that you will answer these questions only from the standpoint of actual reality, not from the "pseudo-reality" at all. Okay?

How powerful are you?

How completely are you to be trusted?

How "necessary" is it that you compromise with "pseudo-reality"?

How many other people do you actually need to have in agreement with you before you can *initiate* the actions necessary to save the world and lead a fully-proud and powerful life yourself?

Additional Reports on "Reality Agreement" Counseling

The "Reality Agreement" approach to counseling continues to be a live, active frontier. It has been taken up more quickly and used with more success and enthusiasm than any previous advance in our counseling practice. Not everyone has been willing to try it, of course, even where it has been explained carefully, but in these instances the hesitation seems to be based on fears, rooted in past experiences, that this approach could turn into an unthinking "formula." (There have been some other specific resistances which also seem rooted in past distress.) With careful discussion and encouragement I think all people will eventually find ways of trying this that will be acceptable to the individuals who now hesitate to use it. My judgment, at this point, is that this approach will eventually have good effects on everyone's counseling.

Many people have written to express opinions that the Reality Agreement approach is only a logical offshoot of some previous developments in counseling. "This is just another way of putting attention away from distress." "This is a way of contradicting all distress at once." "This is a way of getting the counselor's role back to that of listening instead of giving directions that the client probably doesn't need."

Appeared in **Present Time** No. 95, April 1994.

I think these analyses and suggestions are probably all "true." I think, however, that there is some kind of a qualitative shift involved with use of the Reality Agreement approach (when it works well) that can give us a better picture of our real nature and functioning than we've usually until now been able to glimpse through the murk of patterns and patterned activity. Just as "holding directions" between sessions first enabled clients to resist the re-assertion of the chronic pattern, so the keeping or re-establishing the agreement on the fundamental distinction between reality and pseudo-reality *and the persistent effort to think and speak from reality only* seems sufficient to produce continuing and reoccurring discharge.

During the long development of counseling theory and practice, I have persistently tried to find ways to motivate a client *to act* against such deeply installed chronic patterns as those which enforce timidity, irresponsibility, and powerlessness. I have shamelessly experimented with sarcasm, embarrassment, and use of other fears to try to motivate the client to contradict these heavy chronics, since rational appeals usually seemed to have little effect. (Success with this has *not* been overwhelming.) All along it has seemed true that rational motivations would be far more effective than such trying to contradict one pattern with another. The intelligence of the client is certainly where the real power lies. The apparent "effectiveness" and "power" of a pattern can only be a borrowed bit of the actual power *of the intelligence* being held hostage by the pattern.

Now some things have happened with the Reality Agreement that encourage and excite me greatly. A number of clients from many different backgrounds have agreed on the absolute distinction between the reality of the Universe and the "pseudo-reality." They have also agreed on an absolute distinction between the real nature of the client and the pseudo-reality which has been projected at him or at her. On agreeing to this distinction, these clients have immediately begun to discharge. They did this without any questions or prompting from the counselor. With the counselor remaining silent, or at most offering encouragement to the client, they continued to discharge.

If we collect these clients' communications of what it seemed to them they were doing during this spontaneous activity, I think we may be able to learn and communicate to each other some remarkably effective ways for the re-emergence process to proceed.

Even more exciting to me are two experiences that I had with *strangers*. These people did not know me, knew nothing of Co-Counseling, and seemed to have the usual kind of conditioned inhibitions about discharge.

Yet, after brief discussion, they expressed agreement with the distinction between actual reality and "pseudo-reality." They at least agreed that it was an "interesting idea." At that point, *without any further communication between us*, they proceeded to discharge. Every minute or two, their eyes would catch mine. Sometimes they would mention briefly what seemed to them to be "funny," or what seemed "moving." They would then resume discharge, at least as effectively as any of the RC leaders have done with this Reality Agreement approach.

Why does this excite me? It seems to me this opens the possibility of unleashing re-emergence on a wide, public scale. If some of us can find our way enough out of our remaining timidity and shyness patterns to do this, we can show people how they can begin to dramatically change their lives without the awkwardness, confusion, or delays that we old-timers have settled for with previous techniques.

Figuring Out How to Use It

I've had an interesting turn-around with the Reality Agreement recently. I started using it in my sessions shortly after reading about it in the July 1993 *Present Time*. Intellectually, it made a lot of sense to me, and I was curious and eager to try it. However, I did not discharge as easily with the Reality Agreement as I did in my other sessions. I felt that while it seemed to make a great deal of sense, this particular technique was of limited value to me.

About one month ago, due to the gentle insistence of one of my counselors, I decided to take as much time in my session as I needed to answer the questions and to think about the difference between reality and pseudo-reality. Two distinct images emerged in my mind. I imagined reality to be a beautiful planet full of color and warmth. I am sitting in the center of this planet, very calm, at peace and loving everyone and everything deeply. Pseudo-reality, in contrast, is a lightless, bleak planet where I am feeling alone and miserable. As soon as I came up with these visualizations, discharge came copiously.

It was necessary to make the Reality Agreement my own for it to work well for me. The advantages are that I can now easily enter into the agreement with my counselor, as well as have productive sessions. Furthermore, if I begin to feel distressed as I go about my day, I can quickly refer to my "reality planet" and have it guide me to a more flexible way of thinking about my situation.

I have also had some very good sessions by myself using my own version of the Reality Agreement. I imagine my reality planet and then ask myself, "How good are you?" etc. I emerge from these solo sessions feeling a bit more prepared to face challenges.

I am sure there are as many ways to look at the Reality Agreement as there are RCers using it. One of my Co-Counselors told me that whenever he begins to get distressed and is unable to take a session immediately, he simply stops and says, "Reality check!" This, he says, effectively pushes him out of his distress and into present time until he can get a session.

The experience of discovering a way to make the Reality Agreement work for me has been a big contradiction to isolation. I had seen this technique work well for others while feeling, "Oh, this won't work for me. I must be different from everyone else." In fact, it does work! I just needed to figure out how to make it workable for me. I would be very interested to continue hearing from others about their work with the Reality Agreement.

Louise Le Bourgeois
Chicago, Illinois, USA

This list of statements made from pseudo-reality and true reality was worked out in a class near Oxford, England.

PSEUDO-REALITY—*"I am alone."*

REALITY—

•I *was* alone. • I've got lots of friends. • I have only to ask for help. • I've got a loving family. • The world is full of potential allies. • There's a world full of people on the end of the phone, and they're probably going to ring me. • The love of those who died is always with me. • People are just delighted to be in touch with me. • The real me is always connected with the real everybody else—and that can't ever change!

PSEUDO-REALITY—*"The past has made me what I am."*
"I am completely shaped by my past."

REALITY—

•I am completely free to choose. • My attention is in present time. • I learn (and always have) from what happened to me. • Past distresses have no power of their own, except what I choose to give them. • Only my patterns are shaped by my past distresses.

PSEUDO-REALITY—*"I am a victim"*

REALITY—

•I *felt* like a victim. • I have complete power. • I am a conqueror. • I am in charge. • It's my world. • I was pushed into a victim role. (It was my best choice at the time.)

PSEUDO-REALITY—*"I am hurt."*
"I am damaged."

REALITY—

•I can heal. • I am whole—always have been and always will be! • I am completely un-damaged! • I *felt* hurt—and may still feel hurt. • The hurt came from outside, and was put upon me, but it isn't actually me.

PSEUDO-REALITY—*"I am scared."*
"My world is frightening."

REALITY—

•I *was* scared. • I was feeling scared and confused. • I am completely safe. • Most of the 'badness' of 'bad' things is our fear.

IT'S WORKING FOR ME

As I counsel, I am more and more convinced that the reality agreement works. I don't even want to counsel any other way most of the time. It also seems that the more I look at this, the more apparent it becomes that almost ALL of what I have called "thought" is recording. If I counsel about my past hurts I have a pull to stab myself, numb out, etc., even after the session. If I counsel using the reality agreement, my body aches during the session but I don't have a pull to hurt myself after the session. I think that for the most part we have been very confused, even in counseling. In the past we have figured out where the client was restimulated, got them to discharge in the middle of being restimulated (for example, my mom beat me—wa, wa), and thought we were being good counselors and clients because we got an hour of discharge.

One of the problems that I have had with counseling all these years was that it was so depressing to always focus on past hurts—blah. Or after sessions I would be pulled to act out in ways that were hurtful or destructive to me—even though I thought I had made a decision—not to drink, smoke, scream at my girls, etc. After sessions in reality I don't feel that pull—the new pull is to complete health and well-being. This may be boring news to you by now, but it's all very exciting to me.

When I first got into counseling, one of the attractions was the promise, belief, that it is entirely possible to recover from past hurts. And what I saw was people counseling forever and ever—and I thought, "Oh, god, but I want a life." But I was willing to keep counseling. With the use of the reality agreement I actually get more life—my writing is taking off incredibly, my friendships are changing to include more and more powerful people who actually enjoy life and laugh at life. I have more beauty in my life—pretty things. My sense of humor is coming back. And I'm still not smoking. And I discharge more while doing things—crying while writing, shaking while reading poetry, crying at flowers and sunsets, laughing at all kinds of things.

Marcie Rendon
Minneapolis, Minnesota, USA

Overcoming Resistance To More Direct Re-emergence

I would like to let you know my thinking on working from the reality/pseudo reality perspective. I was amazed at the fury that I felt when my regular Co-Counsellor, who had taken on the direction with recognition and relief, warmly invited me to give it a whirl. The resistance I felt was enormous, and I debated quite convincingly for some time though I recognised that stubbornness as a very old recording.

The distresses that appear to be restimulated for me are:

(a) thinking that I'll never get anyone to listen again to how difficult it has been for me and therefore I'll never clear it up;

(b) the sorrow and the pain in having given up on the notion of goodness and rightness in the world. I always thought that I had adopted the idea of benign reality as the most rational perspective to have on existence but that I had never believed in it. The direction held onto by a counsellor who didn't lose sight of it, brought up the grief of knowing that I did believe—or had once.

For the past year or so I have experienced heavy terror restimulation that has come up in a variety of different physical and emotional forms. One of the roots has turned out to be sexual abuse by a member of my family. Working directly on the abuse in a systematic way has been productive, but the restimulation has been, at times, excessive. When one of my regular counsellors asked Harvey at a recent workshop if what we were doing made the best sense, he said it didn't. Now, when I can remember the decision, I use my session time on what is going well.

Lesley Chandler
London, England

It Really Works

I'm sticking with this Reality Agreement. It works much better than running myself into the ground, even if I discharge while I do. This really works! It helps me discharge profoundly and reminds me to repeat it when I feel awful about myself. It actually keeps me in touch with the reality of myself much more of the time now. It forces reality to creep into my mind, and I'm aware of making a decision to keep it in my mind and push the other stuff aside. I think it's a very profound insight and technique—it seems pretty advanced to me, and I'm curious to see if beginning students can practice it without running into pretense or numbness. I guess that depends on how good we are at communicating the idea and counseling people on it.

Ellie Marsh
Albany, New York, USA

An Exciting New Counseling Approach

Reflecting on the counseling approach which involves the client repeatedly asking "Why do you love me, counselor?" has opened a whole new vista of actual counseling with attention away from distress. No distress is alluded to in the client's question, or in the very occasional answers which the counselor may make. It has also become plain in practice that it is the *question* that provides the discharge, not the *answers* from the counselor (which in many circumstances never take place if the client is encouraged to pursue her or his own thoughts as he or she discharges).

The best explanation for this that I have been able to formulate is that the picture that each of us evolves of our relationship to other intelligent humans (probably resulting from our inspection of our own natures as we develop prenatally) is an expectation of being the object of love and affection *from all other intelligences.* What happened at birth (or sometimes before) in the usual (in this oppressive society) "routine" treatment of newborns (and almost systematically afterwards) installed hurts. These hurts quickly became chronic. With the repeated reinforcement of these, I think that almost all of us have lived in deep chronic patterns of *not believing we are loved* for the rest of our lives to date.

Appeared in **Present Time** No. 96, July 1994.

We certainly have made mighty efforts to regain touch with that lost concept of universally-available affection. To try to regain touch with it, we have relied on fantasies, tried "falling in love," used the stirrings of sexual feelings (whether brought on prematurely by sexual abuse when children or by "normal" development during adolescence), read romantic literature, or pursued any other possible source. Many of us have become "stuck" in the pursuit of any of these substitute channels that seemed to offer hope of access to the universal affection that we longed for. The illusions and disappointments that followed have reinforced the barrier.

I think what happens with the simple repeated question is that the wording of the question, "*Why* do you love me, Counselor?", leads the client to *assume* that the counselor loves him or loves her before the client's patterns have become alerted and erected barriers against such an assumption. What happens then is that the barrier between the reality that we have so passionately longed for and our intelligence turns out to be not a "heavy wall of stone" but a thin (albeit tough) film which is pierced by the assumption in the question that the counselor does love us. This contact with reality can lead immediately to heavy discharge which can continue with encouragement for a long, long time. (I do not know of anyone who has continued to use this technique with an aware counselor who has ever "run out of" discharge.)

SOMETHING SIMILAR, BUT DIFFERENT

The new approach I want to tell you about is somewhat reminiscent of this "repeated question" success. I think it can be explained and understood in a somewhat similar way.

I think that all of us developed an expectation (as we grew pre-natally) that we would enjoy *closeness* with other intelligences as part of the normal living of an entity such as ourselves. (This has certainly been occasionally reinforced by the presence of a twin sharing our pre-natal environment with us.) *This* expectation was cruelly denied, too, by the circumstances attending the usual birth procedures and the ridiculous, inhuman separation and calloused treatment given us by the people attending our births. Medical examinations, "periodic" feeding, lack of touch, isolation, interference with the crucially-necessary discharge of the hurts incurred during birth, and other factors, tended to make these hurts, too, a basis for a very heavy and rapidly-deepening chronic pattern.

I will describe elsewhere and some other time the details of how this new counseling approach or "technique" came to light. Essentially the process consists of having the client say to me (or, hopefully, to any other counselor, using that other counselor's name), "You and me, Harvey," repeating the phrase a number of times and telling me the thoughts that come to mind. Discharge almost always begins at once. I have been able to encourage it to start where it is slow by asking the client to add the words, "completely close" to the "you and me, Harvey," and to deepen the discharge after a few minutes by adding the word, "forever," so that the repeated thought (and sometimes repeatedly-voiced phrase) is, "You and me, Harvey, completely close, forever."

I have at this point been trying it for about three months, mostly on the phone, with people scattered around the world in different Communities (also at two workshops and in person with a few people I work with locally). The amount and kind of discharge varies from client to client, but it is usually very substantial and can include heavy sobbing, shaking, laughing, and deep, deep yawns. (I have not been "tantrumed" at yet, but I am sure that it is possible that will occur.)

People in general express great relief at the session. They often volunteer that they have "longed" for such a relationship with me. They describe a feeling of general relaxation, both physical and emotional, taking place. They seem to sense the results of the session as a profound experience.

IT AFFECTS THE COUNSELOR, TOO

This counseling approach is unusual in my experience in the sense that it has an effect upon me, the counselor, very similar to the effect it has upon the client. Apparently "sharing" and "closeness" *are necessarily* two-way experiences. I am finding my own thinking about the availability of closeness changing as rapidly as the apparent changes in the thinking of my clients.

Some of the clients have said (as my clients have often done in the past after successful sessions with me), "This works because I'm doing it with you, Harvey." They say, "I've always wanted to feel close to you. You've been very important to me for a long while, although you haven't seemed able to realize it." At this point, I do not argue with the people who say this. Perhaps I have played a better role with many people than I have been able to credit because of my own heavy chronic patterns of rejection and isolation. I am trying to believe these things they say and accept them as useful contradictions to the negative chronic attitudes that I had acquired from early rejections, political persecution, physical beatings, etc.

However, I do not think this works only *with me as a counselor, or will only work with me.* (In fact, now, in June 1994, I have already heard from a hundred other counselors for whom this approach is working elegantly.)

I think there is a *general* desire of *everybody* to be *close to every other human being*. I think that for the counselor to offer this phrase with his or her own name in it is a reassurance (which he or she can quickly add to) that this closeness is available with this counselor. I frequently attempt to re-laxedly reassure my clients that this is the closeness that I want with them, remind them of the "completely close" and "forever" parts of the phrase (which they sometimes tend to leave off), and I offer a formal agreement that we will be completely close in the future. Sometimes I offer a handshake to "seal the bargain."

When I have worked with the same client more than once, the contact sometimes seems to become faded between ses-sions. It may take several repetitions of the phrases before meaningful contact is re-established and discharge begins again. The effect, however, seems to be cumulative from session to session once the contact is restored.

Work on this approach is, of course, only just beginning, but what is happening seems exciting enough and rewarding enough for me to spread the word immediately and urge people to begin to use this regularly.

The Complete Goodness
of Reality

Our understanding of and our use of the counseling process (the contradicting, discharging, re-emerging process) has been progressing by leaps and bounds. Substantial numbers of experienced counselors have been taking charge of their lives, handling and triumphing in many difficult and challenging situations, and gaining wide influence and leadership in the process.

Individuals new to Co-Counseling are quickly grasping the advanced techniques and approaches, from the literature and from the instructions and modelling of the successful experienced leaders. There are many signs that in the future re-emergence will not have to be a laborious, difficult procedure as it has often been in the first forty-four years of RC. The last four major advances in techniques (the Exchange of Roles, the "Why do you love me, counselor?", the Reality Agreement, and the "You and me, Elizabeth") have changed the atmosphere in our organized Communities dramatically.

The general understanding that discharge takes place whenever a distress pattern is "contradicted" sufficiently and that "contradiction" consists of anything that allows the client to view the distress as *not* present time reality provides a never-ending stream of effective techniques in every Co-

Appeared in **Present Time** No. 96, July 1994.

Counseling (or living) situation where it is applied. From this, we can, at this point, generalize that the *basic* contradiction, which is at the heart of every *useful* contradiction, is the contradiction between *reality* and the great mass of recordings which constitute *pseudo-reality*, whether this pseudo-reality is embodied in the distress recordings and "feelings" of an individual, in false information, or in any of the oppressive functionings of a world-wide oppressive society. This insight becomes explored in the successful operation of "Reality Agreement" counseling. I propose that we extend this exploration further by reference to, and use of, one of the basic insights of our theory.

We have announced, and to some extent have proclaimed, this basic insight over a period of many years. I do not think we have until now grasped and *employed* it to the extent that is useful. This insight is the one which has resolved the "ancient philosophical dilemma" of <u>Determinism versus Free Will.</u>

On the issue of determinism versus free will, there is no general description of reality which can apply accurately to both the past and the future. The ever-moving line of present time divides the past and the future inexorably into two domains which are forever separate. The future is the domain of free will, the past is completely determined.

Everything in the past is determined. Nothing in the past can be altered. It *was* the way it *was*. It is sealed forever in inexorable completion. No matter how the feelings of our undischarged painful emotion recordings may yearn to change the past, *it cannot be changed*.

(The ever-moving instant of "present time" offers free choices and moves us along with this ever-present free choice into the future. If we failed to make the free choice that we now (painful-emotionally) wish we had, the new present instant still allows it in some form or other.)

We may feel (and "think" we think) that the past (immutable, fixed) was "bad," but the truth of the matter has to be that the past *was just fine in every way*. It *was* the way it *was*. It *happened* and therefore it is necessarily *completely acceptable*. All our mental exercises in regretting it, "condemning" it, etc. are simply expressions of our understandably confused attempts to find some way to discharge the emotional distress which has stuck to us in the form of "congealed past pretending to still be present."

I think if we can make direct contact *awarely* with this necessarily excellent nature of the past, the discharge process will be able to accelerate. We already have examples of Co-Counselors acting brilliantly, successfully, and creatively while at the same time discharging voluminously. It has been established that it is *possible* to think brilliantly, act successfully and creatively, re-evaluate, *and discharge* in one big, ongoing process.

I do not yet know how to do this in a way that I can communicate to you, the reader, with any detailed instructions. I may never be able to tell anyone how to reach this point in such a manner. I can, and do, however, suggest that *it is possible*. I can share these insights as far as I have developed them with you, the reader, and I can tell you that I am approximating this process for short periods as a logical outcome of my previously-established directions for re-emergence.

Everything of the past was and is fine. It happened the way it happened. Therefore, it follows inevitably in logic that it happened the way it *had to* happen. If it had to happen, and happened, it is completely acceptable, deserving of no regret. If someone whom we have loved has died, for example, that is just fine. We may need to say "goodbye" to that person a hundred thousand times in session as a means of shedding all the tears that must be shed before our mind can accept reality and be at ease with that reality, but we may be able to speed the process by facing clearly the fact that our feelings of distress *are* pseudo-reality. We may need to face, for example, that all we ever "possessed" of the departed beloved was the information about him or about her which was contained in our memories of that person. We have all that information still with us (once the occluding grief is out of the way) and that the actual "companionship" with that person, which is available in the continuing information we have about him or about her, cannot be destroyed, cannot be lost, and can become and be kept unoccluded.

Our entire pasts are completely satisfactory, completely fine, completely enjoyable. Our ever-moving present is filled with complete freedom of choice. Our entire future deserves delighted anticipation of the sort which we observe in a well-treated, healthy two-year-old who "cannot wait to get out of bed in the morning because there is so much delightful living to do."

Advanced Counseling Is Becoming Simplified Counseling

The newer techniques of Co-Counseling continue to suggest simplifications of the process.

I recently spent some time with a counseling leader. We had no previously prepared agenda. She had arrived on time for a meeting of leaders when the others were all delayed by transportation difficulties. When we had greeted each other and I had invited her to "bring me up to date" about her life, she enthusiastically told me of her two-year-old grandson. He, she said, loved her deeply. Whenever they met she said he would rush toward her calling out her name happily and hugging her enthusiastically. As she told me this she began to laugh freely.

I remembered some of our experiences using the Reality Agreement, times when clients had kept discharging for a long time without any overt intervention from the counselor. This happened after they had made an agreement to think from, and answer questions from, the viewpoint of actual reality as distinct from the pseudo-reality of patterns and distress. Her grandson's love for her seemed a clear expression of reality.

I asked her grandson's name. She told me. I asked if she would try leaning back with her eyes closed, and if she would

Appeared in **Present Time** No. 97, October 1994.

agree to silently think to herself her grandson's name every time she stopped discharging. She agreed.

What followed was two and a half hours of excellent and easy spontaneous discharge. She laughed steadily for twenty minutes, paused for a few seconds, cried freely for ten minutes, was quiet for perhaps thirty seconds, laughed for a long spell, was quiet and looked thoughtful for a minute, then yawned ten or twelve times.

For about two and a half hours she discharged steadily with no overt communication between us, although I am sure she took it for granted that I was still there. When another leader arrived for the last hour, I asked the client to stick with what she was doing. I gave the new arrival a quick, low-voiced explanation of what had been going on. The client continued to discharge, switching occasionally from one type of discharge to another, until the other leaders arrived. At that point I asked her to end the session so we could start the planned meeting.

I was very impressed as I watched this session. The thought kept coming to me that "this is the way counseling is supposed to work."

It seemed like the best functioning of Reality Agreement counseling. Apparently, to think of her grandchild's name was to remind her of actual reality enough to contradict whatever distress came to mind as she cliented. It seemed as if her intelligence was handing up for discharge exactly the distresses that could be processed in that situation with the resources available there.

I have since thought of this experience as a possible window into more efficient re-emergence for all of us to use.

I have set up similar situations with other clients and have usually had success. The (to me) amazing eagerness of people to use the "You and me, Counselor" for heavy discharge has led me to ask some people to use that phrase as their "reality reminder." Most clients who have tried this have been able to do it. When it works, the client is apparently self-directed for long periods of continuously-flowing discharge, switching the kind of discharge between laughter, trembling, tears, and yawning at their own choice.

I have not yet tried this with people who have no knowledge of or experience with Co-Counseling, but I am eager to try it.

I encourage *you* to try it. I will appreciate your reports on how it works.

These glimpses into the possibilities of more efficient use of counseling time and counseling relationships are appearing as a logical outcome of previous steps forward in understanding the counseling process. Ever since counseling began, there have been sporadic individual "breakthroughs" which have encouraged hard thinking and experimentation towards accelerating the re-emergence process.

Many of you have had the experience of a client showing up for a session and being so eager and ready to discharge that greetings and any amenities were bypassed, and the client simply discharged steadily as long as the time permitted. We have sometimes referred to these occurrences as "taking advantage of a crisis" or "things being accidentally just right."

I have told many classes and workshops about the man who came in for his "free" interview for one-way professional counseling some forty years ago. He began to talk guardedly while looking at the floor, looked up into my eyes once and apparently noticed that I was really paying attention to him, and *cried violently for the next fourteen hours.*

There are other phenomena that have kept tantalizing us with the possibility of more rapid re-emergence. One of them is the spontaneous, several-days-long intense discharge and intense re-evaluation that has occurred many times when a Co-Counseling client "turns a big corner" in re-emergence from one of the large and early chronic patterns that had previously dominated his or her life. These clients report days and nights of excited re-evaluation. They tell you that they are re-thinking all the decisions which they had made in the past years which had been influenced by the chronic pattern, that they can feel this re-thinking going on in their sleep as well as in their waking hours.

Something which I know has been experienced by several dozen Community members, because I have personally observed the experience, has happened when a client, carrying a load of embarrassment, such as our society tends to install upon every young person, begins to discharge the embarrassment well. This usually happens in a workshop demonstration. A skillful and experienced counselor reminds the client that full discharge of this embarrassment is very much in the client's interest, therefore the client would never rationally stop the laughter as long as there is more embarrassment to discharge. The counselor reminds the client that if the discharge is interrupted, it necessarily has to be a pattern operating, otherwise the client would laugh persistently until all the embarrassment was discharged.

Since such a pattern inevitably has a vocal component, the counselor is able to draw attention to the sound of this component, and by copying the noise and thereby drawing the client's attention to it, can re-trigger the laughter discharge by copying it each time the noise is made. By the counselor persisting in this copying, the client himself or herself eventually becomes aware of the noise each time he or she makes the sound. Noticing the sound triggers the restarting of the laughter. Many clients, given this much support and awareness, have laughed all that day, all that night, and all the next day. This greatly reduces their total accumulation of embarrassment.

I become excited again whenever I'm reminded, or remind myself, of these glimpses we have gotten and are now getting, more dependably than ever, of the possibility of direct, rapid re-emergence. I would love to hear your experiences, your thinking, and your speculations in this direction.

Was (Is?) the Past Completely Good?

The responses to the article, "The Complete Goodness of Reality" in the July, 1994 *Present Time* have been many and varied.

First contact with the proposed ideas seldom brought enthusiastic agreement. In some of the workshops to which I presented the ideas in the article I asked for the workshop attendees to address the questions in lengthy mini-sessions immediately afterwards. After the mini-sessions, when people were asked to raise their hands if they easily agreed with the ideas in the article, only one or two hands would be raised. The rest would indicate they did not yet agree, or that they weren't sure whether they agreed or not. All participants in the mini-sessions, however, seemed to discharge profusely during their turns in the mini-sessions.

Many people later wrote to me. Some said they were now understanding the issues better. A few indicated they now agreed. Many had more questions to be resolved.

The most common disagreement was with the statement that "The past *was just fine in every way.*" Some wrote, "How could you say that the Holocaust was fine?," or "Don't try to tell me that *my* childhood was fine!" One said, "You've urged us to be realistic; it feels like realism to me that the death of my children was *bad.*"

Appeared in **Present Time** No. 98, January 1995.

What seems to me useful (in a counseling sense) about the proposal that past reality is completely good is that it can guide us and encourage us to discharge completely the distress left by the past events and come to the relaxed, rational view of the events which had previously felt distressing. In that sense I think almost everyone will come to agreement with the proposal eventually. I think that they will be helped to discharge the distress left by past events by the theoretical agreement that relaxed acceptance of all the past will inevitably occur with enough discharge. I, myself, intend to pursue this activity persistently. I think that I and other such "pursuers" can demonstrate and share our experiences with others successfully.

Some people took issue with my statement, *"Everything in the past was and is fine.* It happened the way it happened. Therefore, it follows inevitably IN LOGIC that it happened in the way it *had to* happen." These were people who had some knowledge of formal logic, having studied it academically. They felt that I was mis-stating the logic they knew, and therefore coming to an unjustified conclusion.

I think my statement is correct, but I should have said that when in the sentence quoted above I say, "In logic," I am talking about a *corrected* formal logic, corrected from the things we were taught in school. I refer to this correction earlier in the article when I say that earlier thinking in Re-evaluation Counseling had "resolved the 'ancient philosophical dilemma' of <u>*Determinism vs. Free-Will.*</u>" Traditional logicians had always assumed that one could treat the past and the future the same way (a confusion that undoubtedly arose out of the persistence of the distress recordings attached to the logicians) and had left the question of determinism vs. free will an unresolvable dilemma.

Once traditional logic is amended to include our discovery that the past and the future cannot rationally, on this question, be treated as one category, then my use of the phrase "in logic" *does* make sense. Of course I am sure that traditional logic will eventually have to be amended to include this correction, no matter how much discharging traditional logicians will have to do to get up to date.

Information
Which Young People May Find Useful
(pass it on)

You have been misinformed, lied to, deceived about many things.

Young people have been told many things as if these things were true which are *not* true. The basic reason for misinforming young people is to make it possible to use them and their efforts to make profits for the oppressive system and its supposed beneficiaries, the owning class. Excuses for such misinformation are used such as "the truth would be too hard for young people to understand," or "these (wrong) ideas will make people cooperative," or "we need to scare them so they won't dare to rebel," or "we have to tell them things that will make it easier to handle them."

Much of this misinformation is "hallowed" in that it has been repeated over and over for generations until "everybody" takes it for granted.

Many of these lies are invalidating of young people; that is, if believed, they will make young people think badly of themselves, not have much confidence in themselves, not trust each other or cooperate with each other.

From the World Conference of Young People, Surrey, England, July 20, 1994.

Some of the truths that we have, so far, been able to separate from the lies, truths which contradict this misinformation, follow below.

You are a *good* person.

All human beings are basically *good* people. They do not always act as if they were good (you may not always have acted as if you were good), but there is an understandable reason for people acting badly. When people have acted badly, it has not been their fault. Sometimes people have acted badly out of ignorance, and as soon as they have had correct information they have changed the way they act and then act as good persons. Most of the time when people act badly it is because something happened to them in the past which hurt them and left a recording in their minds which kept them from being intelligent in that kind of a situation when it happened again. The bad recording in their minds pushed them to do bad things of the sort that had happened or had been done to them when the recording in their minds was made.

No matter how people seem to defend such old recordings, they are eager to become free of them. People who use Re-evaluation Counseling are learning how to help each other become free of such recordings.

In particular, *you* are a *good* person.

You are very intelligent.

All human beings are intelligent. As people learn to uncover all their intelligence from the distress recordings that have concealed part of it, they discover that they are so intelligent and function so intelligently that people could correctly consider them geniuses or *potential* geniuses (as they have considered Madame Curie, Leonardo da Vinci, Albert Einstein, and Nelson Mandela geniuses in the past).

Your mind is able to handle more information more accurately than all the computers in the world could handle if they all acted together. Computer experts have estimated that such a mind as yours can and does handle eleven trillion (11,000,000,000,000) items of information every second in ordinary living.

Our intelligence arises out of the great complexity of our central nervous systems which allows the complexity of our thinking to reach the level of *free choice*. From the present moment, looking forward to the future, *we can decide any question which we will face any way we want to and any time we want to*. We do not ever again have to do as we are told, or accept another's decisions without thinking for ourselves.

You are very intelligent. You have the thinking capacity of a genius.

You are eager to like and be close to all other humans. All other humans are eager to like you and be close to you.

Part of our fundamental nature, which developed spontaneously before we were born, is to expect to be loved by all other intelligences because we are intelligent and because we love all other intelligences. Another part of our fundamental nature, also developing before we were born, is to desire to be close to all other intelligences and expect them to desire to be close to us.

These expectations are interrupted by mistreatment before, during, or after our births and are replaced by the appearance of, and feelings of, not being loved, not being close to, closeness to us not being desired.

Some current developments of counseling include such approaches as the client repeatedly asking the counselor, "Why do you love me, counselor?" and also the "You and me, counselor. Completely close. Forever." These are uncovering the reality of and the practical re-attainment of the universal hope that surrounds us of all other people loving us, wanting to be loved by us, wanting to have closeness to them accepted by us, and wanting us to be close to them.

You live in a good, friendly universe. It is, overall, benign in its attitude toward you.

Our universe has been changing and evolving for about fifteen billion years since its beginning. Living things have been evolving on our planet for over three billion years. Thinking creatures similar to ourselves have been evolving for at least a million years. Humans *of our species* have been living for at least a hundred thousand years. During these long stretches of time, we and the universe have evolved to fit each other well. We fit this universe well and have freedom and power to modify it to make it fit us better.

Everything in the universe tends, on the one hand, to become more complex, more satisfying, more interesting. We have called this tendency in the universe the "Upward Trend" because this tendency is useful and interesting to us as humans. Everything in the universe is also pulled toward uniformity, toward simplification, toward the destruction of complexity, toward monotony. We have called this tendency the "Downward Trend," but we recognize that both trends operate everywhere on everything and that the processes of the downward trend fuel or lend strength to the processes of the upward trend. Neither trend is "bad" in itself.

We, and particularly our intelligences, occupy a very high, continually ascending position within the upward trend of the universe. We may be, and certainly are close to being, at the very tip of the ascending upward trend. For this reason, new complexities, new creativities, new ideas, new inventions please and interest us mightily, but we have no conflict with the downward trend that surrounds and supports the upward trend. We simply try to keep the downward trend from "leaking into," "slopping over into," or otherwise interfering with the operation of the upward trend.

In this sense, we are the caretakers and custodians of all other forms of life. They are the reservoir of growing complexity out of which our own greater complexity has emerged.

Our *inherent goodness* arises out of the nature of the reality of the universe of which we are a part.

The past cannot be changed.

The past *was* the way it *was*. We may have to discharge a great deal to feel comfortable about accepting the past, but it will turn out to have been acceptable all the time we were having difficulty accepting it.

We have been thinking intelligently since before we were born.

We began thinking in an intelligent way some months before we were born. We did not "become intelligent" only after we were born. We did not "become intelligent" at any later period in our life though we have been lied to about this in many ways by the oppressive society. We have *always* been very intelligent since our central nervous systems developed before we were born.

We need enormous amounts of information for our intelligence to work well. We enjoy acquiring this information. We began acquiring this information before we were born and spent all the time when we were babies and young children acquiring this information as rapidly as we had the opportunity. All of us fully used every opportunity we had to "learn something new."

Play, which is often treated by the distress patterns of the oppressive society as if it were "amusement" or "entertainment" or even "wasting time," is a very basic, profound, and effective learning process. Young people who are allowed to play together without mistreatment and given access to information learn very, very rapidly. People who have thought well and deeply about these questions have concluded that any happy, well-loved, and well-supported children, given enough of a chance to learn enough information in interesting ways, could easily learn and speak several languages and have a "Ph.D." in any subject that interested them by the time they were eight or nine or ten years old. (An occasional child, under accidentally lucky circumstances, occasionally does this.) This capacity exists in every one of us still.

Oppressive societies never work well for people and always collapse. The present society is in the process of collapsing.

About six thousand years ago societies that forced most people to become *slaves* and be owned by a small number of *slaveowners* began. These societies began collapsing about two thousand years ago and were replaced by societies in which a few people were *nobles* and everyone else worked for them as *serfs*. Serfs were not owned outright but were exploited to produce wealth for the nobles. A few hundred years ago those societies were replaced by our present societies. In these, a small number of people, the owning class, *own* all the means of production (with this ownership often concealed through the mechanism of *corporations*) and most people, if they can find jobs, work to produce wealth for the owning class. These people, the working class and the "middle class," receive only a part of the value they produce. This is paid to them as *wages* or *salaries*.

"Greed," the urge to have more, to own more, to take away from other people what they had and own it for oneself, became the overriding patterned motivation that was encouraged by the oppressive societies.

The owning-class-working-class societies are currently in crisis everywhere and are breaking down all over the world.

Every young person alive at this point will participate in the future changes which will replace the existing societies with some kind of a cooperative society. The existing societies and all their institutions (such as governments, schools, newspapers, television) deny that this is happening, but it *is* happening anyway. Young people need to be prepared for this.

The adults among whom we live, including our parents, are essentially very good people, but most of them were treated very badly as young people and were told that the way they were treated is how young people *should* be treated.

The adult humans around us are good, intelligent people who have been hurt in so many ways that their goodness and intelligence have often become concealed. They often do not seem to be good or intelligent because they are covered with distress patterns. Their goodness and intelligence still exists, however, and with intelligent effort and assistance from outside can be regained on the operating level.

The adults around us have been mistreated in many ways when they were very young and as they were growing up. This is because the hurtful societies in which they have lived were dominated by distress patterns rather than by the intelligence of people. People became hurt more and more systematically in the ways that would lead them to "fit into" the society, rather than left functioning in ways that were sensible and useful and would be good for their children and other young people.

They were mostly "trained" to believe and do everything the oppressive societies told them to believe and do. Because of the resulting distress patterns they find it very hard to think differently than that and tend to treat young people the way they were treated. This is the main reason why you have had "trouble" with the adults around you while you were growing up. Parents and teachers are generally afraid to treat young people more sensibly than they were treated when they were young, and the institutions of the oppressive societies have always tended to criticize them and threaten them if they act intelligently toward you.

If your parents have begun to learn and use Re-evaluation Counseling you are fortunate. That may make things much easier for you to live well and to recover all your intelligence, your independence, your courage, and your power. However, even the best of parents or family members who have used Re-evaluation Counseling, and use it, will probably still have many distress patterns operating, and it will continue to take courage and persistence for you to establish a cooperative and mutually helpful relationship with them such as you would like to have. It is best not to be discouraged by the difficulties, however. You should persist.

Any differences between people—differences in age, gender, skin color, language, ethnic background, or size—are trivial and unimportant. The intelligence of every individual establishes an overwhelming *commonality* between all humans.

The intelligence of every individual enables all human beings to work closely together, assist each other in attaining their goals (both the goals they hold in common and their individual goals), enjoy each other hugely, reach out together for good relations and unity with all the people that they can make contact with, and plan and achieve a decent society in the future.

The oppressive society uses many weapons to try to prevent people from uniting and cooperating with each other.

The oppressive society and its institutions try to train people, beginning when they are very young and naturally trusting, to believe false information. The oppressive society and its institutions try to convince young people that they should discriminate against other people and mistreat them for any differences from themselves—differences in age, gender, language, skin color, and any distress patterns which have been installed in the past. Other differences attempted to be used in this way include differences in cultures and differences in sources of income (that is, whether the income is received from ownership, from wage work, or from salaried work). The oppressive society will use any difference it can as an excuse for oppression and disunity.

Young people intuitively resent these separations which the society tries to install and intuitively wish to enjoy contact with each other across *all* differences. Young people will always *want to respond* to a good program of unity with *all* other young people and with *all* humans.

Addictive, mind-blocking, mood-altering "drugs" are systematically used by the oppressive societies to keep people from thinking, organizing, and effectively defending and advancing their own interests. Young people are especially targeted and made victims of these substances, and then blamed, punished, and attacked for being victims.

There are many varieties of chemical substances which, if taken into the body, can create temporary illusions of "well-being" but which interfere with the intelligence and functioning of people and leave distress recordings whose effect is to compel the continued use of these substances in an addictive way. These substances are often given glamorous reputations by the people who make them, sell them, prescribe them, and make money from them in various ways, but all of them are harmful substances that keep people from thinking well about themselves or acting well in support of each other. People can become "addicted" to any of these substances. This simply means that their use produces patterns of hurt, which interfere with the person's intelligent attempts to not use them, by acute internal discomfort if the person attempts to withdraw from their use. Alcohol, tobacco, cocaine, heroin, marijuana, many sedatives and "exciters," and "mood-changing" drugs of all sorts are the enemies of all excellent human functioning. Young people can support each other in avoiding becoming addicted to these and can help each other through the "withdrawal" discomforts of breaking any addictions that have been started, by standing by and helping each other discharge until the compulsion feelings in the distress recording are completely erased.

Similar addictions to harmful "comforts" are produced by coffee, tea, various drugs included in soft drinks such as colas, excess sugar, fatty food, etc.

The oppressive society insists, through its institutions, that the intelligent thinking of young people is "naive," "unrealistic," and incorrect, and that getting older ("seasoning," "maturing") is what will lead young people to intelligent agreement with the program of the society. This is a *lie*. It is the *intensive hurting* of young people and the resulting installation of patterns on them while they are becoming adults which is the actual source of most adults' submission to, and cooperation with, oppressive activities.

To submit to the enforcement of oppressive ideas will spoil your life. Young people can resist this "training" and act together to *change* the society and *interrupt* the spreading of oppressive ideas to other young people.

All of you young people will be "in charge" of the society in a much shorter time than you are usually realistically aware of.

It is only a very short time until you presently-young people will be "grown up." Even with the existing attitudes of the oppressive society, you, as adults, will be in a position to claim the right to change things so that everybody's lives can become enjoyable, so that intelligence can determine how the society operates. You will be able to successfully insist that the world be used for enjoyment and elegant survival instead of for greedy profit-making.

You young people have the opportunity to make firm contacts and dependable relationships with each other now, using the time and opportunities available to you while you are still young. If you do, these contacts and agreements can, within a very few years, become a powerful central force for great "people's movements." These movements can end all oppression, end all discrimination and mistreatment of people by each other. They can end the threat of overpopulation of our planet. They can guarantee the survival of all species of living things in our world. These movements can explore the universe. They can prepare to establish frontiers for human populations on the moon and on other planets, and eventually, in other star systems.

You will find yourself, in practice, delighted with how boldly and swiftly and successfully you can take charge of the world situation. You will find that you are more than powerful enough to prevent unnecessary damage to humans and to the world of living things and the millions of species which comprise it. You will find that you can easily prevent any further damage to the lands, the forests, the oceans, and the atmosphere from taking place.

Overpopulation can be easily halted by making information about and technology for contraception available to all peoples. The terrible waste of earth's greatest treasure through the extinction of species of living things can be completely ended. Adequate resources towards research and organization for public health and survival can lead to the elimination of AIDS or any other of the "doomsday diseases" that are likely to develop in our huge human populations. The oceans and atmosphere will quickly heal themselves if we end the abuse caused by the society's profit-seeking pollution.

Move boldly while you are young. Challenge the adults to follow your lead.

A Year of Continental and World Conferences

We are just back from the World Conference of the Re-evaluation Counseling Communities. Plans were worked out, and committed to, by representatives of people from all over the world.

There were four Continental Conferences held before the World Conference, one in Australia, one for North and South America, one for Africa, Europe, and the Middle East, and one for Asia. Then, the elected delegates from these four Continental Conferences came to northern California in November and gathered in a big grove of redwood trees to finalize some of the decisions of the world-wide Community.

This society is crumbling very rapidly. The rising stock exchange prices are no indication of stability. The amount of unemployment is spiraling upwards rapidly. Even though RCers may not have been as deeply bothered by what is going on as the general population (because of the large component of middle-class people in United States RC where so much of the RC population is still concentrated), a great portion of the population of the world is in deep personal economic trouble and already enduring suffering at the present moment. The conditioned passivity, the training to "put up with things," the attitude of "hoping something will be better next week,"

From a talk at the New England Teachers' and Leaders' Workshop, held at Prindle Pond, Massachusetts, USA on December 12, 1993.

is still holding the population passive, but there will necessarily be violent upheavals soon. Times of struggle are closer to us than we are accustomed to noticing. The economic situations we face are very threatening.

NO MORE WORLD WARS, NO NUCLEAR HOLOCAUSTS

There are positive aspects to the present, however. We are safe from any more *world* wars at this point. The population of the world has made up its collective mind against world wars. Local wars are still being pushed as hard as they can be in many places, but they will not be escalated into world wars. The last big attempt to do so was the Gulf War. It was called off as a result of sheer terror on the part of the managing division of the world owning class as they glimpsed the risk of what would happen as the population began to move to reject the war.

The threat of nuclear holocaust, as it was being deliberately prepared by the competition between two great imperialist powers, is no longer present. The danger *was* very real, and we had no way of knowing that it would be eliminated, but that threat, the big threat of nuclear holocaust, is no longer present. We're not in danger of total nuclear disaster. We are not in danger of another *world* war.

THE RE-EMERGENCE OF INTELLIGENCE

Possibilities seem to be opening for a rapid climb of humanity out of the confused mess that has accumulated upon our species over its entire existence.

There are many, many workshops like this being held around the world. RC is functioning, to some extent, in over seventy countries and is spreading rapidly. The possibility of rapid re-emergence is there.

We in RC are still stuck in a general condition of timidity. Many of the people that I know well at this workshop are very smart. They have a good grasp on theory. They are learning rapidly. It hasn't yet occurred to them, however, in any meaningful way, that they personally can do something decisive about the general condition of the world. They are still waiting for something to happen or for somebody else to take decisive action.

There is no one else who is particularly qualified to take decisive, overall responsible action to change the world. If an unknown someone acts, it will be, to a large extent, accidental. You in this room, however, if you turn one particular little corner in your counseling, if you discharge hard, primarily as a result of making a certain decision, you *are* in a position to change the face of this world very rapidly. You can save scores of millions of lives, maybe hundreds of millions of lives, in the process and open the door to the kind of living on this planet that we have dreamed of since we have existed.

Some good things have been happening. The grapevine has quickly passed the word around about the Reality Agreement way of counseling, for example.

We have some reason to be proud of the progress of counseling. We have used the "Repeated Question" technique in which the client is invited to ask, with a lilt in his or her voice, "Why do you love me, counselor?" For most clients, and particularly with younger people, discharge roars and rages for half-hours and hours at a time. We have found that it goes on working like this when people use it after the workshops where they have first seen it demonstrated.

With this approach we got our first glimpse that profoundly effective discharge was possible without the client paying *any* attention to the distress. It was an almost accidental break away from past techniques. A number of other developments followed, primarily the Reality Agreement. If people actually follow this procedure, when the thoughtful agreement is made and the counselor falls back to the role of being a reminder, the client tends to discharge persistently and changes his or her life very rapidly.

Some other things are happening. The "Why do you love me, counselor?" procedure revealed how close almost any two people are already to a deep, trusting, loving relationship whenever they dare to act on it. This was plain. It showed up in many of the demonstrations that I did. If I asked somebody to ask me, "Why do you love me, Harvey?", often the younger people would discharge for a long, long time without ever asking the question aloud. They simply came to an awareness of something that effectively contradicted heavy distress and allowed voluminous discharge.

It is plain, as person after person tries this, that just under the surface appearances people have a deep confidence in an in-fact loving relationship between *any* two people if they can break through some kind of a (usually unchallenged) "insulating film." Those of you who have seen me do demonstrations on this know that I usually try to flexibly answer the question of why I love them. Once they start discharging, it doesn't seem to matter much what I say. If I say something like, ". . . because you are such a slob," they tend to keep discharging and tell me, "Oh, that is so funny, you are so funny, Harvey. Ha ha." Their security in the relationship that they have broken through to and their contact with me are so deep that *any* words from me tend to be interpreted benignly.

Large numbers of people are now trying to use the Reality Agreement. People hear about it and then try to use it. If they try to use the form and questions but don't actually make the agreement, it doesn't work. But if the agreement is actually understood and made, it works and it works and it works. For some people it provides an immediate, permanent turning point in their lives. If you observe one of these people, who has grasped the concept clearly and who is using it for rapid re-emergence, I think you will get a glimpse of how close all of us are to our actually pristine state. It begins to seem plain that the distress never *really* corroded us, never *really* corrupted us. It deceived us. It smeared our appearance. It deceived us about each other. Yet we are beginning to see clearly that all of us are still just as good as we ever were. It is a simple, short path to get the reality of ourselves back, to have the kind of life that we want.

I note two developments with the Reality Agreement that surprise and excite me. One is that a certain number of clients who are new to its use begin to discharge without any questions from me (as the counselor), as soon as they have understood and committed themselves to keeping actual reality separated in their thinking from the pseudo-reality of the pattern's misinformation, oppression, and confusion. They do not need any urging, permission, or direction from me as a counselor. They furnish it themselves and continue to discharge just through holding to this distinction.

The other development is the result of some attempts by me to ask for agreement, such as I have been seeking with clients, from *total strangers* who I have met in airports. Some of these strangers grasp the concept quickly, make the agreement, and proceed to discharge with delight without any further instruction about the process or explanation of "what discharge is," or any talk of "desired results."

This implies to me that we are working our way into the use of a very basic process which can accelerate not only *our* re-emergence (we determined, committed, dedicated Co-Counselors), but perhaps that of the *whole population* around us.

STILL CAUGHT IN THE COLLAPSING SOCIETY

Of course we are still, at least nominally, caught in the grips of this *extremely* oppressive world-wide society. This society and the patterns which are running it have no ability to care about us or care about our having good lives. They have no ability to care about the incomparably valuable complex of living things on our planet, to care about the beneficent ozone layer shielding us in the upper atmosphere or the lovely environment of our planet in general. Even though any human life is precious beyond belief, this patterned society and the patterns running it cannot even hesitate over ordering the destruction of millions of lives.

Yet this whole vicious complex can continue to operate only because human intelligence has not confronted it firmly. It has no power over us except through our conditioned submission to it. All of us are covered with a general blanket of timidity patterns that we usually don't even realize are there. It doesn't occur to us ordinarily that, at some past times in the history of the world, a few people changed the face of the world as a whole as a result of their individual actions.

Yet the reality has to be that you can make a decisive difference. You can change everything. You are quite capable of simply rejecting what is going on in the oppressive society. Each of you has the possibility of doing this. You just need to "make up your mind" and stick with your decisions, and the whole world will change around you. People *will* come to your support. That support will grow to whatever size is necessary.

Buddha, Mohammed, David, and Jesus made up their minds firmly, and the world around them made major changes.

I think we experienced Co-Counselors are at a similar point. I think it is true of everyone here tonight that if you could find a way to just make up your mind and stay with your mind made up, the world would start changing now, and large numbers of people would rise to support you.

A FRONTIER IN OUR RELATIONSHIPS

Another frontier of re-emergence is opening up for us. I'll mention it now and try to answer questions about it later.

In some ways I have always been quite confused about personal relationships. For example, I have spent my life encased in a total rejection pattern. It began the moment I was born. I have fought to get out of it, but I have always found it very difficult to believe that anybody "liked" me.

I worked hard as a labor organizer and a political organizer and as a founder of RC to try to get people to "like" me. Yet it has been almost impossible for me to believe that anyone did like me. Any beginning belief has tended to be turned off by any of the numerous attacks that have filled my life.

Yet it is now becoming apparent that quite a few people like me. They really do. They like me. They have an enormous amount of goodwill in my direction. I feel safe in saying this. It is hard to find words strong enough for what I am finally having to see. It is not easy to see it, it is not easy to say it.

People in large numbers *adore* me. Can I feel this? Only for brief periods. However, I am a responsible person and a theorist, and so I decided not to forget this but to share the implications of it with you, so *you* can act on it.

I have always been curious about everything. I have been curious about the cults which attract thousands of people, people who sell their houses and give the money to the guru, people who will wash the guru's feet or do anything else he wants them to do. Why do people act this way?

Patterns are certainly involved in the irrational, non-survival parts of these relationships. Patterns are certainly involved in much of the observable "religious" devotion which has been held up to us in the examples of "saints" and others. I doubt, however, that patterns furnish the courage to face death easily, to decline to submit no matter what temptations are offered as rewards. I think there must be a core of fellow-feeling, of devotion to each other as humans, underneath any patterns that have been tacked on by cultist or religious conditioning.

There has been heavy conditioning (and training) of almost all of us to be isolated from other people, to not trust other people, to assume that we must be essentially lonely. I am guessing that behind the rigid shells of the patterns all people are "wildly eager" to be completely close to each other. I am conjecturing that every one of us probably has a deep, deep need to not spend any more of our life isolated and separate.

I think we get little glimpses of this when we "fall in love." I have tried to explore this. I look over there at you and I fall in love with you. I just fell in love with you a minute ago. I am betting that this "falling in love" is just a hole punched in a screen that, up to now, has "lonely-ed" our separate lives.

Some of us *are* getting close. I am getting close—very, very close. I have spent much of the time in this last period thinking about this development. Some of you already know what I'm talking about. I can tell by your eyes that you are thinking with me. I don't know that anybody ever thought what I'm thinking before, or in as earnest a way as I'm trying to think. I think that we are very near to being able to be completely close to each other without exception. We are very near to being able to live "madly" in love with each other, without any "religious" patterns attached, without any "gurus" to lead us, and without embarrassment. I think we are close to understanding that this is our real nature, that the isolation never was intended to be any part of us.

Many of us, I think, are ready to fall completely, permanently in love with each other. I think so. I see three or four faces here that have broken through years of circling me but never getting close, who recently became close. You know something? I am just as close to them as they are close to me. It feels exactly right. Solid. I will never have to be concerned about that person's relationship with me, even if I never see him or her again. This is a solid reality that we are getting ready to enter.

To make the breakthrough we will need some of our familiar techniques. We will have to contradict and discharge sexism. We will have to contradict and discharge racism. We will have to contradict and discharge the adult oppression directed at young people. We will have to succeed with every liberation struggle. Nothing we have learned about counseling is going to be useless. At different times each familiar technique will become useful. I think, however, that we are getting ready to make a direct breakthrough.

A series of discoveries have led up to this expected break-through. The Exchange of Roles highlighted the central importance of contradiction of the distress. The "Why do you love me, counselor?" was a surprising spin-off from that. There is no distress involved in that at all. Yet people have discharged day after day for weeks using it. Then came the Reality Agreement, the agreement to answer questions only from reality. I have been using this ever since I first tried it in April. I worked on it with Dan and Beth. We had a day together before the workshop and accidentally tried it and it simply worked. It worked so good we kept on doing it. We've been doing it ever since at every conference and workshop.

It is time for a whole bunch of us to decide to give up all paying-attention-to-distress, to entirely give up paying attention to distress. We now have the techniques for doing that. In the last *Present Time* and in the last International Reference Person's letter I conjectured that we are now hot on the track of a very ancient mistake. Quite a number of us have re-emerged far enough that we are getting a glimpse of how good life can be, but then inevitably wonder how our species could have dug ourselves so deeply into the pile-up of distress. How could we have killed each other off in endless wars? How could we have almost assembled an "inevitable" nuclear holocaust? How can we go on destroying all the forests, ruining the air? How could our species, which we know from many samples is very smart and is very good, do these things?

My guess is that somewhere back there our ancestors ran into problems dealing with the environment outside of themselves. They tried to pay attention to the problems, to pay a lot of attention to the problems, to think about them as much as they could and keep working at them until they eventually came up with a solution. If the problem was objective, in the real world, the more they thought about it, and the more attention they paid to it, the better the chance was that they would solve it.

Our remote ancestors in this sub-species of ours were apparently very much like we are. They were vulnerable to distress patterns. Accidents would happen and the discharge would not be complete and they would be left with patterns.

Or *contagion* would operate. Somebody else's pattern would come over and do an injury to them, and that would leave a recording on them. It must have happened at least these two ways. Even though the current biggest source of distress patterns (which is *oppression*) didn't get started until seven or eight thousand years ago, patterns must have been installed by accident or contagion at the very beginnings of our species.

Our ancestors were probably enough like us that, through introspection or some other way, they noticed that there was something wrong. They noticed that they weren't thinking as well as they had been. They weren't enjoying life the way they had previously. Something was wrong. So, borrowing the method they had found for solving a problem in the objective world, they tried to solve the problems left in themselves by patterns in the same way, that is, by putting attention on them, by thinking about them. That would be an understandable mistake a hundred thousand years ago, wouldn't it? Perfectly understandable. Unfortunately, we are learning that, except under special circumstances, unless you have somebody else paying you attention, unless discharge is encouraged, unless someone stands by and insists that you discharge *enough*, you don't solve *internalized* problems, *patterned* problems, by paying attention to them. What happens if you simply pay attention to a problem that is "inside you," is that the problem "gets" you. You get a new layer of distress every time you think about it.

I think this is a fairly good guess as to why this wonderful species of ours that is so capable of being completely wise, completely loving, completely positive, taking care of the environment so wonderfully, slid into this miserable pre-history and history of passing on patterns. We did this at first by accident and contagion and finally, in the last several thousand years or so, by systematically trapping ourselves into societies that impose patterns "deliberately," cruelly and viciously, on and on and on, just to keep the irrational society going.

Thank you for listening.

Excerpts from Letters to RC Leaders

Remember that RC today is different than it was even six months ago. Remember that the RC that you have learned in the past has necessarily included some of the patterns of the people you learned it from and that we must continually sort out the essential RC from the patterns that attach to it.

RC is the best approximation that we have achieved at any one time to the hitherto obscured reality of the nature of the universe, the real nature of human beings, and the process of re-emergence of the real nature of human beings from the obscuring distress patterns, misinformation, and oppression.

PREFACE TO "WHO'S IN CHARGE?"

Up from inanimate, out of one-celledness,
Gaining complexity, structure, and plan,
Changing, evolving at last to intelligence,
Maturing, we make it to Woman or Man.

The struggle, repeating each fresh generation,
Exposes each one to distresses and pain.
When healing is blocked then illusions anachronate
Delude us that past situations remain.

Large, we feel little. When safe, we feel threatened.
Informed, we plead ignorance. Free, we hear chains.
Powered, we act helpless. We cling to dependency.
While ours gather dust, we trust someone else's brains.

Idiot societies bully and threaten us,
Herd us through ruts of disaster and blah,
Inflaming our scars to secure our conformity,
Blindness perpetuate, unreason raw.

Once only heroes dared rise up occasionally.
Now, all who read this know how to discharge.
Who guides your steeringwheel? Powerhouse? Universe?
If it's not you, then just WHO IS IN CHARGE?

From *Zest Is Best*

AUGUST, 1988

There are "two groups of distresses" that affect owning-class people because of their class position.

The first group of distresses includes the grief, fear, rage, etc. over having been so tyrannized and mistreated as children, distresses which are felt as hurts and which owning-class people are eager to discharge. The "second group of distresses" are the ones that owning-class people have often become "adjusted to" or have become "comfortable with," such as arrogance, condescension towards other people, self-centeredness, preoccupation with their own roles, and "taking over" in all situations.

MARCH, 1991

THE CONCEPT OF "CONTRADICTION"

One way that the basic importance of the concept of "contradiction" has been highlighted these last few months is by the spectacular success of "exchanging roles" in a session. In such a session the client agrees to, and persists in, threatening the counselor with the hurtful behavior which was turned on her or him in the past. Thus I will ask a client to say to me, "I'm going to hurt you physically, Harvey," and then repeat an unlimited number of times a half-sentence such as, "I'm going to ____" with the client being encouraged to be completely free in what she or he threatens to do to me. Clients who have had great difficulty in discharging on past physical mistreatment, in this format often immediately burst into prolonged laughter after making only one or two threats and proceed rapidly to trembling, shuddering, and shaking interspersed with laughter. This discharge often continues for hours with little or no difficulty. The explanation for the success certainly must lie with the contradiction that is offered by the change of roles. I find that I can enhance the effect by being very cheerful and relaxed, appearing to welcome the threat of injury and being enthusiastic about the creative ways in which the client is threatening to furnish it.

To use the phrases, "I'm going to abuse you sexually, Harvey," and the follow-up, "I'm going to ____" in the same way, is just as spectacularly successful. I have had great successes in proposing other lines of threat tailored to fit the hurts that underlie the client's chronic distress, as well. I do not know as yet whether this works well unless the counselor is relaxed and confident, but I encourage all of you skilled counselors to experiment with it.

The spectacular success with contradicting people's distresses in these simple ways makes me suspect that we have just begun to appreciate the importance of "contradiction." I am hopeful that the next period will see a great surge forward in the effectiveness of our counseling everywhere in the world as a result of following up this concept.

THE COLLAPSING SOCIETY AND ITS WARS

A good deal of our attention in the last few months has been, of course, on the attempt by the collapsing society to get a new world war started over guaranteeing U.S. and Western dominance of the world's largest oil supplies in the Persian Gulf. Now that the active phase of that war is almost halted, we can take great pride in the spontaneous initiative that RC leaders and RC peace activists took almost everywhere to help the basic peace sentiment of the people find expression. In my opinion, the war was halted when it was largely because of the very powerful peace sentiment building up in the United States and in the countries which made up the "Coalition" forces.

The killing, of course, has not ended. The Kurds and the anti-Hussein Iraqis have become the object of a new war which Saddam Hussein seems to have tacit tolerance of the Western leaders to continue.

The inability of the collapsing societies to even *try* to solve their economic failures and conflicts with anything beyond the production of munitions and the launching of wars is becoming plainer all the time. It cannot help but prove highly educational for the growing peace forces. People can be encouraged and organized to require intelligent solutions for human, economic, and environmental survival. Proposals for new, non-oppressive societies can be thought about and worked out. Tim has proposed, and I heartily second, the idea of organizing special widespread discussions by RCers and their friends on what a new non-oppressive society can be like and will be like and possible steps for getting there after thorough, widespread, world-wide discussions.

LENDING LIBRARIES

Spending Outreach Funds for scholarships and transportation costs to bring people from new Communities to workshops has certainly worked out well. We will continue to do this and hopefully expand the scale of our efforts in this direction as far as the shaky economic situation permits.

There are some indications that the money spent on lending libraries, to establish access to the wealth of RC literature in every new Community, has even greater long-range effect. It has always been a small portion of active RCers who have been able to attend workshops on anything but a local level, and the literature has shown its ability to greatly excite people all by itself. There is a growing network of "literature enthusiasts" who are able to infect the people around them with eager excitement about what they read in the RC books, journals, and pamphlets and what they see and hear on the audio and video cassettes. We have established several score of such lending libraries to date, mostly in places remote from the older Communities or countries where RC has been functioning for some time. I think we will put more effort and resource in the direction of a much larger number of such lending libraries for the next year and see if we do not obtain much faster growth in the Communities where such lending libraries are established.

To the Communities that are already large and well-functioning, I propose that you use your Outreach Funds to establish such a lending library and publicize it within the Community. The cost will probably be about $750 (US).

To new, small Communities I propose the following steps, which will be considered a requirement for International Outreach subsidizing a lending library:

(1) that an RCer at an available location (residence, store, office, or other) undertake responsibility for keeping the literature and tapes in order and available with at least some hours every week when people can visit and check out the material they wish to use (signing for the literature and promising a return date);

(2) that the Communities commit themselves to adding new publications to the lending library as they are published so that the lending library stays up-to-date (where the economic situation requires International Outreach for this to happen, that the local Community be responsible for applying for Outreach and seeing that the literature is ordered);

(3) that the library include one copy of everything that has been published in English so far and is still in print, and one copy of each available translation in other languages that are in common use where the library is located, and that these translations be specifically asked for in the application for the library;

(4) that applications for such lending libraries be directed to me in my capacity as International Reference Person.

NOVEMBER, 1992

1. The final collapse of the presently-world-wide owning-class/working-class society is well underway, and it is unlikely that this society can recover its functioning enough to achieve any stability in the future.

2. The collapsing society itself will make every effort to force the working classes and the ordinary people to bear the

cost of the accumulated exploitation and mismanagement. In spite of the conditioning of people to believe classist nonsense, it is becoming clearer to many that it is no longer possible for humanity to function under a "profit system."

It is, however, the society that is collapsing, *not the people, not humankind*. This society has always been our enemy, an oppressive entity. It is finally becoming unable to function even in its old ways. Its collapse is providing us with the opportunity to set up rational economic and social relationships between us.

3. The RC Communities have fought our way to our present clarity about reality, and have survived and established firm roots in many locations of the earth (RC is functioning to some extent in sixty-six countries). We can take assurance, confidence, and satisfaction in how well we have done in spite of the inevitable mistakes that accompany such an effort.

4. It is time for the RC Communities to function even more effectively and efficiently. We have worked out *Guidelines* which summarize the workable ways of relating to each other and operating as a Community. It is time to grow consistently *and rapidly*. Growth should be a characteristic of every support group, every class, every Area, every leaders' group, every Region, and every workshop.

5. An entirely new level of RC based on *taking responsibility for everything around us* needs to be "extruded" from the existing Communities. This new level will consist of people who "take responsibility for everything" and who move to change everything that is wrong. These people will act spontaneously as they become aware of anything that needs changing. They will act on their own initiatives. They will

organize support for themselves among the people whom they lead and wherever they take responsibility.

To do this is apparently going to require the discharge of powerlessness patterns with which we were all saddled very early in our lives.

We now have ways of bringing these formerly "invisible" patterns into visibility. We have the beginnings of techniques which can thrust people into persisting contradiction of these patterns and lead to profound and continuing discharge.

Members of the RC Communities are not automatically expected to function on this new level of RC. It must be each person's own choice and decision. I expect that many of the existing *leaders* of RC will be eager for a chance to make this choice. We also have some experiences already indicating that many quite new RCers are able to grasp and move on this concept well (if they are given *unremitting* insistence from the person who is counseling them).

The message of their patterns to most Co-Counselors is that contradicting more than one pattern or more than one part of a pattern would be unbearably uncomfortable. This is not true. It is actually not a bit more uncomfortable to contradict every single pattern one has *at the same time* than it is to contradict any part of any pattern. The client might as well contradict all distresses at once and move determinedly into fully rational behavior, rapidly and effectively.

Another useful commitment that helps "roll up" and discharge the entire fabric of invalidations, internalized put-downs, and similar difficulties is to coach the client to say in a voice of excited discovery, "It *has* to be true that I am *completely all right!*" followed by, "It *has* to be true that I have *always been completely all right!"* followed by such words to the counselor or listener as, "No wonder you're impressed by me!"

OCTOBER, 1993

WORLD SITUATION

The situation in the world currently is very hard on working-class and other low-income people but is a situation offering great opportunities for world changing. It is a time when RC thinking and policies can quickly become widely accepted.

The contemptible motivations which have always guided the governments of the leading powers of the world are being exposed more and more rapidly. The striking advances in communication through satellites, cable, cellular phones, and computing networks are creating an informed population. The old methods of oppression in secrecy cannot cope with this. (Of course the oppressive society attempts to misuse these new information channels *also* for misinformation and oppression.)

The old "psychologies" are bankrupt. The current results of classist oppression and the breakdown of society are immediate and devastating. The costs of this press heavily upon working people everywhere with unemployment, hunger, health difficulties, and demoralization. However, the ruling circles of the present societies are themselves terrified, and, behind their bluster, have no ideas of what to do about this general collapse beyond desperately competing with each other for the shrinking profits.

We in RC, of course, also feel the economic pressure. We are having a tough time but probably, in general, are surviving better than the populations around us just because of our better-informed status and our greater flexibility in the face of crises. For our personal interests, however, as well as for the interests of the general population, we need to break through the timidity and passivity which have been conditioned upon us as part of the general population. We need to meet together and discuss our current situations with each other. We need to face the fact that things will not "get better" on their own. Only bold, innovative initiatives and determined struggle can bring an end to the deterioration of living standards, environmental quality, and health care.

POLITICAL SITUATIONS

It is becoming increasingly clear that the so-called "liberal" victory in the United States elections was, as usual, the election of people who are also dominated by the centers of financial power in the United States. There is some hope for a major improvement in the terrible state of national health care, but the weakness of the labor movement and its failure to take demanding initiatives leaves the lower-income majority of the country in increasingly worsening situations. Because of the United States' dominant imperialist position, the deterioration here has immediate and vast negative repercussions around the world.

The current struggles in Russia reflect the confusion which counterposes political freedom and sensible economics. One leader promises political freedom but no economic security. The other group needs economic security for survival but is partly led by old bureaucrats who are associated with the special privileges of the former party bureaucracy. The word is badly needed that being able to deal with patterns makes the co-existence of economic democracy and political democracy possible.

The signing of the peace accord between Israel and Palestine, while only a beginning step, is a completely positive development.

The need for international working-class unity is becoming more and more apparent.

THE "REALITY AGREEMENT"

The discovery that agreement between the counselor and the client to examine the client's nature and performance only from the standpoint of reality (excluding the "pseudo-reality" that has usually dominated our interactions) is revolutionizing counseling. Discharge is becoming profound and continuous. (See the July and October 1993 *Present Times* for details.)

The repercussions are also profound. A quote from the October *Present Time*, page 7:

"We may here be uncovering the tracks of a very ancient human mistake. If this is true, this mistake has side-tracked and distorted human progress for a long period of time.

Other species of humans besides our own have lived in the past. We are sure of their existence because of fossil remains. All present humans, however, are members of one very closely related sub-species. . . .

If the earliest members of our sub-species were as much like ourselves as the available evidence indicates, they certainly were vulnerable to being hurt physically and emotionally. This means that they were vulnerable to acquiring patterns, by accident or by contagion, even though the principal current mechanism for installing patterns—oppression—was still a long way in the future.

Once a distress pattern was installed upon them, these forebears of ours must have noticed, perhaps from introspection, that part of themselves (their humanness and their intelligence) was not working as well as it had before the hurtful experience. They undoubtedly tried to do something about it.

If they responded in the way in which they had learned to deal with other difficulties in their lives, they undoubtedly tried to "take a look at" the phenomenon, "think about it" and "find a solution." It seems probable that this is just what our forebears did. For them and for us, when we have an objective problem outside of ourselves to be dealt with, the more attention we pay to it, the more we think about it, the more likely we are to find a solution.

Unfortunately, as I think we are finally coming to clearly understand, <u>putting attention on a problem caused by a pattern</u> only helps in very special circumstances, that is, when someone else will pay attention to us, when discharge is permitted and encouraged, and when some motivation to persist in the process is furnished. <u>To pay attention to a problem caused by a pattern in usual circumstances</u> is to become victimized by the pattern, to have it extend its sway over us, to add another layer of distress to the pattern for each time we try to deal with it in this way. Dealing well with a problem caused by a pattern involves <u>not</u> putting one's thoughtful attention on it, involves placing one's attention <u>away</u> from the distress and on information that <u>contradicts</u> the distress, involves taking an attitude that refuses to identify a pattern with oneself."

APRIL, 1994

COUNSELING ADVANCES

The "Reality Agreement" approach to counseling continues to bear fruit wherever it is used. It apparently is remembered and used more widely than any previous advance in counseling. You will find a report on developments with it in the April *Present Time*. I will mention here just a couple of points that seem to me significant information and progress.

Both of these apparently involve the inherent *spontaneity* of the process. In the beginning of Reality Agreement counseling, the agreement between the counselor and the client was plainly of great importance, but the technique seemed to lead to discharge only on questions asked *by* the counselor *of* the client. More recently, it has been noticeable that *making* the agreement by the client has in many cases spontaneously started continuing discharge. The client did not always need the guidance of the counselor's questions ("How good are you?" "How innocent are you?" "How intelligent are you?", etc.). The client's *agreement* to think only from a position of reality itself seemed sufficient to launch his or her mind on a discharge-producing survey of his or her own thoughts. With other clients, the counselor's questions have seemed necessary to start the process. The indications are, however, that this spontaneous capacity to review the accumulation of patterns and discharge in a free, ongoing manner probably exists for everyone and can be used very effectively once it is uncovered.

The second development is even more exciting to me. (I have had a limited number of opportunities to try this so far because of the pressure of health and work.) I have had a few opportunities to approach *complete strangers* (strangers to me, strangers to the value of the discharge process, strangers to counseling or counseling theory), with the essence of the Reality Agreement. In two cases spectacular results were forthcoming.

I explained my proposal that actual reality and the pseudo-reality are fundamentally distinct from each other and then asked if they agreed with me about this. They asked for clarification a few times and then stated that they *were* in agreement with me about that. Then, without any further action on my part, they began to discharge and continued discharging. Sometimes they paused to explain "what was so funny" or "what moved them so" and then resumed discharging. Sometimes they didn't bother to explain but simply continued to discharge.

These occurrences excite me greatly. They seem to me to offer hope that perhaps with our present gains and understanding we can learn to skip the sometimes tortuous processes that we present Co-Counselors seemed to have had to go through to reach our present level of competence in Co-Counseling, discharge, and re-evaluation. Perhaps we can introduce new people to the process and ourselves "get on with it" in an accelerated fashion, just by *concentrating on* and *using* the distinction between reality and pseudo-reality.

(Jenny Sazama, the International Liberation Reference Person for Young Adults, writes from Boston that young street people that she works with in her day-to-day job have incorporated this distinction into their street language. They say to each other, in rejecting statements which they feel are not true, "That's a pseudo.")

REASONS FOR *GUIDELINES* REQUIREMENTS

I have noticed confusion recently, in some correspondence, about people issuing statements or publications which purport to speak as "RC" or *represent* RC policy. There has also been some confusion about activities for raising (and using) "RC money" or "money for RC projects."

The *Guidelines* provide that any statement or publication that purports to speak for RC, or represent RC as such, that is circulated within the neighborhood of a particular organized

Area must be approved by the Area Reference Person before it is issued. This includes Area newsletters, leaflets, and announcements. Any publications that are circulated on a wider scale than within the neighborhood of one organized Area, need to be approved by the International Reference Person before they are issued and circulated. (This includes all special publications of any sort that circulate beyond the confines of one neighborhood.)

A limited, careful exception to this is allowed only for the newsletters of Information Coordinators. The circulation of these newsletters is restricted to the people *who actually write items for the newsletter*, so that the newsletter in effect is a simple way of exchanging individual letters between the members of that group. These Information Coordinators' newsletters are not permitted to be circulated to any other people. Thus they are just opinions of the individuals who "write to each other" through that limited newsletter. In all other cases, it is a general requirement under the *Guidelines* that a responsible leader of the Community, either an Area Reference Person or the International Reference Person, takes responsibility for the accuracy of what is said in any publications.

The International Reference Person may designate another person to review and okay certain particular publications, thus acting as a deputy to the International Reference Person, but the responsibility for what is published after such review remains with the International Reference Person. (For example, this is done sometimes in a newly-developing Region where a temporary Regional publication [Regional publications are not part of our structure] may be supervised or edited temporarily by someone designated by the International Reference Person. Such arrangements are temporary and last only until organized Areas have been set up and

Area publications can exist, or until translation of the existing International literature has progressed far enough, in the case of difference in languages.)

THE REASON FOR SUCH CARE

The reason for this care and caution and for insistence on adherence to the *Guidelines* in this respect arises out of the distinctive character of RC theory and practice and the importance of distinguishing it from the patterns which generally operate in society. Our growing body of "RC knowledge" is sharply different from the mass of patterned assumptions on which the societies operate and with which people everywhere have been deluged in the process of their training and conditioning by the oppressive society.

It is a crucial and important step for all RCers to learn to "think for themselves," to "trust their own judgments," to "act independently." Everyone must be free to make their own mistakes and recover from them. This is an important part of our progress. Where we are acting together as a group, however, to reveal the actual reality of ourselves and the world and clear it from the patterned misinformation and lies which have distorted and concealed it so thoroughly in the past, we need to act carefully and together. It is important that we not blur the distinctions or repeat any of the old confusions when we offer information about "RC" or for "RC." We must protect and share the gains and clarity which we have made and exchanged with each other. This is why we have "rules" and limitations on who can "speak for RC."

We have many leaders and careful thinkers who, if they were to issue written statements or speak publicly "for RC," would probably represent RC very accurately, at least most of the time. If, however, they do not follow the *Guidelines* and follow the careful procedures that have been worked out for keeping our policies consistent and our voice a united one, they will appear to others to set a precedent. This precedent will be claimed by others who are not as careful, thoughtful, or well-informed, for issuing "their version of RC" which can, in all innocence, be deeply patterned, misleading, and confusing.

Quite a number of RCers have built or become leaders of wide-world organizations where they speak out freely for these organizations and offer policy on behalf of these organizations. Such leaders, in general, are very careful to distinguish what they say as leaders of these wide-world organizations from what they say as "leaders of RC."

The only problem that has arisen around RCers who lead wide-world organizations is the occasional careless use of the RC Community to circulate the publications which they have written and published in their wide-world organizations within the RC Communities. This, in general, is *not* a good idea because the publications have not passed the critical process for being circulated in RC, and this misuse of the RC Community for such circulation in effect violates the "no socializing" principle which is so important for the functioning of the Communities.

It is good that people are excited at finding they are competent at writing good articles. It is true that achieving publication for one's article in the RC journals, books, or pamphlets is sometimes slow to occur. (Our growing Communities increase our work load, and the economic distress arising from the society's collapse limits our financing.) It is worthwhile waiting for RC official approval and Rational Island publication of your thoughts and creativity, however.

THE HANDLING OF FINANCES

Some of you are also feeling that it is onerous to have to handle finances through the Outreach accounts of the Areas or the International Community, whether these accounts are handled through Personal Counselors or the Re-evaluation Foundation (or in the case of Areas outside the United States by special legal arrangements within the country where the Area exists). Impatience is sometimes expressed at having to write grant applications, at having to get approval for them from the Area Reference Person or the International Reference Person, and at having to account for the ways the money was spent. People who become excited about a particular project often propose to set up special funds for that project and are reluctant to have to include these funds as part of the regular Outreach Funds.

In practice, however, our financial dealings must be capable of being audited and approved under the strictest procedures, and only the Foundation and Personal Counselors Inc. actually keep correct enough records and have them reviewed to make sure of compliance with existing laws and good accounting practices. Here, too, "impatience with procedure" is understandable but no excuse for carelessness with correctness. We cannot afford to cut corners and subsidize transportation and fees for workshops directly from the workshop funds. Instead, all such Outreach subsidies must be handled correctly through the Outreach Funds and grants. We must keep books and render accountings to these responsible structures in all that we do.

The purpose of our Outreach accounts is to provide new people financial assistance when they could not otherwise participate in Re-evaluation Counseling enough to decide to join Co-Counseling or not. Financial assistance has in the past been offered to people of oppressed groups, whose incomes tend to be very low because of the oppression, and to people in locations remote from existing Communities who need financial assistance with their transportation costs in order to come to a workshop conducted by the existing Communities. Rarely, assistance with the workshop fees and transportation costs has been furnished to individuals who seem so admirably qualified for leadership within the Communities that we are motivated to provide every possible assistance to expedite their participation.

In general, Outreach assistance does not continue past the time when the person has had an adequate introduction to RC theory and practice. If the group the person belongs to has too inadequate an income to participate in traditional middle-class workshops, the job of the Community and the new RCers is to plan and organize workshops on a level that fits the living situation of the new group (for example, monthly workshops or classes for working-class people on Saturdays or Sundays, small workshops in homes to avoid the rental expense of a hall, use of local churches, etc., etc.). The occasional practice in the past of middle-class groups subsidizing people of color or working-class people to attend workshops and classes indefinitely in order to maintain a pretentious "appearance" of having attracted and integrated with themselves people of color and working-class people, has largely been eliminated. It should be *totally* a thing of the past. As people of color and working-class people increasingly take leadership and initiative and come to dominate the Communities, these mispractices will naturally be eliminated.

At the last World Conference the *Guidelines* were modified to allow for the fact that in this oppressive society certain sections of our populations are *permanently* denied access to incomes which would allow them to share the expenses of classes, workshops, and other activities in RC. Some such groups are very young people (infants or pre-school children), children of elementary school age, young teenagers, young black men in the United States, severely physically-disabled people, severely genetically-disabled people (Down's Syndrome), people incapacitated by advanced age or chronic illness, etc. With these populations in mind, Proposal 45 in the new *Guidelines* says of the use of Outreach Funds, "These funds may also be used for the purpose of equalizing to some extent the opportunities available to people whose inherent situations make it necessary to have assistance for full participation in Re-evaluation Counseling activities."

FEBRUARY, 1995

CAN WE USEFULLY THINK OF HUMANS AS "COMPOSITES"?

I am trying to think of a more useful viewpoint to govern my relation as a human to other humans. One approach I am thinking about is to regard myself and all other humans as "composites." One part of this human/pattern composite would be the basic natural and intelligent human (as we RCers are sure that we all started out to be). This human part of the composite is intelligent, good, powerful, responsible, courageous, kindly, and *committed to cooperation* between humans. The patterned part of the composite is the sum total of the false information and the patterned behavior left by hurts, by the internalized oppression, and by the "submission to oppression" left attached to the person.

Thinking of oneself as first person singular, one's own job might be thought of as double-barreled, i.e., relating to both parts of the other person's composite. Awarely, one would know that these two entities are present and that each must be dealt with. Can we work out a strategy that calls forth the human side of the other person and puts one's own human side forward to cooperate with it and enjoy it, *and at the same time* remember that a completely different "set of tools" is necessary to deal with the patterned part of the composite? The tools and attitudes with which one will relate to the human side of one's associates will be consistent with each other and enjoyable. The tools with which one must deal with the bundle of patterns which is masquerading as part of the person will necessarily be of great variety because of the great variety of the patterns that must be dealt with.

I think we have all had a few experiences of converting a person functioning in the grip of a dramatization into someone who begins functioning rationally, cooperatively, and with appreciation for the intervention. What I am trying to think my way to here is some kind of a beginning description of a "generalized" way to accomplish this. Can we profitably think of ourselves as viewing the other person through a kind of "pair of binoculars" in which we can see and pay attention to the view through one lens of the *excellent intelligent person* and at the same time see, through the other lens, the dramatizing pattern for what *it* is? Can we skillfully reach the human and establish communication with her or him and *at the same time* contradict the "acting out pattern" as we observe it through our other lens?

I'm sure my initial difficulty in doing this, or the initial difficulty of anyone else who attempts to do this, will be the pull of *my own* distress or the *client's own* distress to focus on the patterned behavior as if it were the person or even to allow a patterned response of one's own to develop to the "composite" person as a whole.

We are already working in this direction in our attempts to improve our effectiveness in the Counselor role and we *do* have examples from our experiences where this has successfully taken place.

I will let you know of any successes I have or any insights that I gain. Please share your successes or insights as you try this. Share them with me as well.

REMEMBERING TO CHALLENGE A BASIC CONFUSION

Our non-human ancestors necessarily, in the absence of intelligence, relied upon their *feelings* to guide them in their actions. They also relied upon the concurrent possibility of their inherited patterns of behavior being modified by experiences containing tension. (In the same way, distress patterns are imposed upon *us contemporary humans* by experiences of tension.) Such *acting on the basis of feelings* remains *possible* for us, their intelligent descendants.

Statements have been made, repeated, and stressed in our literature that feelings are to be felt, but that only intelligence and logic are suitable *guides to action*. "If the feelings are pleasant, enjoy them, but only act on what you intelligently think. If the feelings are unpleasant, contradict and discharge them, but only act on your logical thinking." This is a crucially necessary attitude for the recovery from addictions. It seems to be widely understood in this context. It also seemed to be more easily understood as long as people were mainly discharging through the shedding of tears.

Now, however, I often hear clients in demonstrations declining or avoiding directions which would otherwise bring discharge by insistently rehearsing that they are "too scared." They say, "That's too scary," or "I'm embarrassed," or "That's embarrassing." Distresses that *could* be rapidly discharged thus continue to dominate clients' activities needlessly and slow discharge down with a persistently rehearsed excuse or dramatization. This dramatization is usually to the effect that to follow a particular direction or action, using a particular tone of voice or a particular facial expression, cannot be carried out or cooperated with because of the "feelings" that doing so brings to the client.

How one *feels*, rationally has nothing to do with how one acts. One can feel "convinced of imminent death" and yet one can act boldly and bravely to do what makes sense. Traditionally we have expected parents to act like this if their children's lives are in danger or seem to be. Some of our earlier cultures held out to us examples of individuals who did this as "heroes" or "heroines" and as the models for the rest of us.

Such "selfless" behavior has become "out of fashion" in today's cultures. We Co-Counselors, however, who have come so far in our quest for rational living, can certainly recall our knowledge of our theory in this respect. We can simply face "feeling" the terror or the embarrassment which is slowing down our counseling (and our clienting) and move rapidly through these levels of distress at speeds far greater than we could move through the earlier heavy levels of grief discharge from which many of us are currently beginning to re-emerge.

Understanding
Relationships
in the Community

A Modern Philosophy

The people who associate themselves with Re-evaluation Coun-seling tend to have certain commonalities in their philosophies and practice. Different individuals speaking out in large conferences tend to recognize each other as "RCers" by the similarities in the ways they think. Out of the constantly growing and evolving "theory" of RC and the practices of RCers a general philosophy is emerging. In any particular instance or group of individuals, patterns are still likely to be involved. This may bring a patterned agreement or a patterned disagreement between their patterns, but there is also an observable tendency toward rational agreement. Below is an attempt to explicitly state some of the widely-agreed-upon characteristics of this commonality of views or philosophy. Readers are invited to respond to this draft with agreements, extensions, objections, and applications.

Philosophies change with realities and have throughout human existence. Operating on an out-of-date philosophy has been the basis for many of the destructive conflicts of the past. Can we summarize a philosophy that will be up-to-date for the present and perhaps even guide us through future confusions as well?

1. A real universe exists.

2. This universe is knowable to any desired degree.

Appeared in **Present Time** No. 91, April 1993.

3. Attaining any particular degree of knowledge of the universe will probably always open new vistas of knowledge to be explored beyond that point.

4. Human intelligence and the concepts and processes which it involves is a possibility implicit in the nature of the universe itself. It is not necessarily the most complex manifestation of the universe, but it is the most complex manifestation that we intelligent humans are as yet in contact with or have knowledge of.

5. We do not need to reject or disown our physical, mammalian, primate nature in order to appreciate, esteem, and advance our intelligent nature. The two natures are completely consistent and without contradiction. In the absence of distress experiences the inherited instinctive patterns of behavior are allowed by the human intelligence to go on functioning in the ways that contribute to the individual's survival *or* are brought under the supervision of the intelligence and are enhanced, modified, or suppressed as the human intelligence decides for the person.

6. The more primitive forms of life are quite mechanical in their interaction with the environment. They respond to the environment in rigid ways which have led to successful survival and reproduction for past generations of their strain of life. Occasionally, through the intervention of chance or accident or through modification of the environment, cosmic radiation, etc., mutations are produced in the nature and functioning of the individual organism. Most such changes lead to non-survival of the changed organism. Occasionally, however, such changes lead to improved functioning of the organism and its descendants and may enable them to cope with changed factors in the environment that were devastating to strains of the organism which did not mutate. This is

the basic and principal mechanism of evolution. Over a long period of time it has produced (from much simpler ancestors) the enormous number of varieties of life now existing on the earth.

7. At some of the more complex (more recent?) evolutionary steps (certainly with mammals, some birds, and some mollusks) a mechanism for modifying the behavior of a single organism (a primitive kind of learning) developed. This has often been called "conditioning." Functioning in this way a creature going through an experience of tension records the perceptions and behavior taking place during the experience. The previously existing patterns of behavior are then replaced with the "recording" of the organism's *actual* functioning during the experience. From then on during similar experiences the individual organism functions on the basis of the recording of how it acted during that tense experience. This recording replaces the previous inherited behavior.

This mechanism, in effect, represents a crude kind of "learning." The new behavior is just as rigid as the inherited behavior which it replaces but may have an improved survival value over the previous behavior. Human beings deliberately use this conditioning to produce changed behavior in domestic animals. They do this by imposing calculated experiences of tension on the animal.

8. Human beings function inherently on their *intelligent* nature but are vulnerable to having it interrupted by an experience of physical or emotional distress. During this period of distress the human being regresses to functioning on the basis of the more primitive mechanisms similar to those used by non-human animals. While this is taking place, the human acts without intelligence or with greatly reduced intelligence and acquires a recording of the more primitive behavior taking place during the time of distress.

When the period of distress is over, intelligent behavior tends to be resumed. Nevertheless, the recording of the distress experience is retained. It can later be triggered and "take over" the behavior and feelings of the individual by a mechanism that we have called "restimulation." Such a "restimulation" can be brought about by a similarity in a new experience to the recorded distress experience of the past. It can also be brought about by a kind of "seeking" by the human's mind to find contradictions to the distress recording. Such a "seeking" is apparently motivated by the individual's desire to bring the rigid recording up against an available series of processes, which can, if assisted correctly, dissolve the distress recording, free the information frozen in it, and free the individual to be once again intelligent and flexible in the area of behavior in which the individual had temporarily become rigid and unintelligent.

9. The vulnerability of human intelligence to this process of acquiring distress patterns and having itself distorted by or replaced by such primitive behavior is a contradiction to our essential nature. We have no way of knowing at this point whether this is an accidentally unfortunate characteristic of human intelligence or whether this is an inevitable stage or consequence that any emerging intelligence or intelligent entity anywhere in the universe would necessarily experience. Nor do we know whether such a non-human intelligence elsewhere in the universe would have to search for and find dependable ways for emerging from such vulnerability the way we have had to do. Nor do we know how difficult it would be for such an intelligence to learn to prevent the acquisition of such rigidities.

10. It has been observed and confirmed by repeated observations that such distress patterns can be acquired by "accidentally" incurred experiences of pain, discomfort, or emotional distress.

11. It has similarly been observed, and the observation confirmed, that a distress pattern can be incurred by one person through that person's vulnerability to a kind of "contagion." In this process the "acting out" of *their* patterns by one or more *other* persons can impose a distress experience *and resulting distress pattern* on the first person.

12. It can be observed and deduced that at some time in the past (at different times in different places, the earliest probably occurring some six thousand years ago) class societies were invented (based on existing patterns of greed and violence). These class societies have systematically imposed and installed distress patterns on all the population in order to achieve the conformity of the humans in the societies to the irrational rigidities of the societies themselves.

13. Human intelligence has found existing processes available, or has evolved new processes, or has modified and converted already-existing processes, for eliminating previously-incurred distress patterns. These processes tend to dissolve distress patterns and liberate intelligence to be once again freely functioning. They free the information, which was previously trapped in the distress pattern, to be available and useful. If these processes are carried through to completion, they will completely erase the effects of a distress pattern and restore the human being to full functioning in every way.

14. The physical activities or manifestations which observably indicate that these re-conversion processes are taking place are outwardly characterized by one or more of the following: tears or sobbing, trembling or shaking, laughter with a cool skin, storming with angry sounds, violent physical movements, laughter with a warm skin, reluctant talk, eager talk, relaxed laughter, yawning, stretching, and scratching. An inclusive name for all these processes is *discharge*.

15. These processes are attempted by all humans as part of their spontaneous and persistent attempts to recover their inherent human functioning. They are often, however, inhibited to varying degrees by the feelings of discomfort which accompany them. They are often also severely inhibited by earlier distress recordings installed on the person when he or she was an infant or child, including threatening or disapproving messages of forbidding or reproaching their discharge.

16. The regimentations of individuals by the installation of distress patterns and by enforcements imposed by oppressive societies and cultures have often been "justified" on the grounds that such conditioning has made humans more effective in their exploitation of the environment. (Such apparent gains, particularly in the expansion of the population, have actually resulted from the improved organization of people, not from their conditioning or oppression.)

Apparent (but only apparent) benefits to the ruling classes of the oppressor societies have included wealth, political power, successful aggression against neighboring societies, and wider domination of other peoples. Even the ruling classes, however, and all other classes obviously, suffer grievous loss of their finest human abilities and their enjoyment of life. Overall, the damage to the humanness of people, to the environment, to the planet, and to humans' understanding of reality, has been severe.

17. The forms of human societies have passed through an evolution, each step of which has contained built-in internal contradictions which eventually have led to the collapse of the particular form of that society. Slaveowner-slave societies gave way to feudal lord-serf societies, which gave way to owning-class-working-class societies. Owning-class-work-

ing-class societies are presently in the process of final collapse from their internal contradictions. Experiments at attempting classless societies (the Paris Commune, the Soviet Union, Chinese Liberation) have failed to succeed permanently (so far) because of the antagonism of the class societies surrounding them and because of the persistence within the attempted new society of distress patterns carried over from the previous class societies. These persisting patterns have often led people who *proclaim* their adherence to the premises of the new society to actually act out the oppression of the past (often in disguised forms) rather than function according to their commitment to the new society.

18. A fundamental oppression involved in all human societies to date is classism. In this oppression, one group of people claims and uses power over all the others in order to take from them the value produced by the others through their effort and labor. The oppressing class leaves the robbed class with just enough of the value they have produced so that they are able to maintain themselves and reproduce new members of their class. This is modified to some extent by assigning a larger share of the produced value than is commonly done, to a small number of individuals from the oppressed class, who are thus bribed to function as a "sub-class" which assists the ruling class to exploit, subjugate, dominate, and control the rest of the oppressed class. This sub-class is sometimes called a "middle class," or a "bureaucracy," or "intellectuals."

The subjugation of the oppressed classes is always basically accomplished by force, violence, and threats of death. Armies are maintained for this purpose, as are police forces, networks of secret agents and informers, prison guards, and supervisors. To such brutal force is added the installation of "traditions of submission," of "holy" awe, myths of "innate" superiority and inferiority, and religious structures which preach the "correctness" of the existing oppressions.

Addictions to "slow" poisons, such as tobacco, alcohol, hemp, narcotics, sedatives, etc. are systematically promulgated among the oppressed people, though often "officially" disapproved of.

What is usually called "education" is added in the form of training and conditioning children and young people to internalize the oppressions being placed upon them by accepting as "correct" the oppression of themselves and of each other. These internalized oppressions include the concept of themselves as inferior or limited or unable to function in anything but their assigned role in the society. They include the concepts of hostility to and competition with any people different from themselves in any recognizable way. These internalized oppressions include attitudes of hopelessness and resignation, and seeing enjoyment of life as only being available in some future existence.

19. The obvious robbery of people by the oppression of classism remains so clear and so obviously damaging to most of the population, in spite of the propaganda and conditioning that promote it and excuse it, that additional mechanisms, which function as "special" oppressions, have been created and perpetuated to maintain the classism itself. Classism continues to exist everywhere in the world only on the basis of dividing the exploited people against each other and "training" (conditioning) them to oppress each other. This is the role of all the subsidiary oppressions of racism, sexism, oppression of young people, anti-Semitism, and the oppressions of older people, disabled people, and people of minority status based on culture, language, and education differences.

Any difference of a group in the population from the majority or "standard" sections of the population is enough of an excuse to allow the creation of one of the subsidiary oppressions which maintain the basic exploitation of classism.

Thus men are conditioned to be sexist toward women, to oppress them and take advantage of them on mythical bases of "inferiority." Adults treat children as "inferiors" to be blamed, harassed, and degraded. Different shades of skin color are used as a basis for the cruelest and crudest exploitation of splendid human beings on the excuse of racism.

Every age group in the population is blamed for some aspect of the general oppression.

The elders are treated as "burdens." People who speak a different language are ostracized. Physically disabled people are discriminated against instead of being supported. People who have been hurt chronically in ways that make it impossible for them to conform to the standard patterned behaviors of the culture are treated as criminals.

20. A rational philosophy would unite all of us in intransigent opposition to *any* form of oppression. We would intuitively organize and persist in overthrowing any oppression directed at ourselves in any role of any kind. We would organize as allies to eliminate the oppression of any group that we observe being subjected to oppression in the society. We would seek out, locate, expose, condemn, and organize the ending of any oppression directed at any group in the population. No oppression would be accepted as too light or too unimportant to bother with. It would become a point of high principle to actively overthrow such organized mistreatment, to seek restitution for losses suffered from past mistreatment, and to bring together all the groups of op-

pressed humans to support each other for the elimination of every kind and trace of oppression. Eventually we would and will end the oppression of classism, which is the source of all the others.

21. Certain positive attitudes arising out of our inherent nature seem to exist spontaneously in all human beings if they are not short-circuited by enforcement or the imposition of distress patterns. These attitudes include enjoyment of other humans. They include enjoyment of activity, communication, touch, physical interaction (games and play), intellectual interaction (conversation, discussion, argument), companionable exploration of new environments, and cooperative modification of the environment to improve the survival potentials of all.

22. At a certain stage of physical development or maturation members of each of the two human genders develop a spontaneous interest in members of the other gender as possible co-participants in sexual activity. Unless the imposition of hurts creates and leaves distress patterns in this area of functioning, such interests and activities remain relaxed and rational.

23. We are learning to appreciate the reality of ourselves as being intelligent without limits. We are developing better understanding of certain aspects of reality. We use these understandings, but we expect to have these current understandings superseded by better understandings. These will come about as the result of wider and more intense experience with reality, as the result of exposure to other people's thinking, and as the result of inevitable, surprising breakthroughs to newer and more profound concepts and views about the reality that we observe. Our emergence from chronic patterns through the processes of discharge will

dramatically change the scope of our intelligence, not only individually, but also for large groups of us.

24. We are confident that we have the potential of being aware of everything that is going on. We seek to expand our degree of awareness and our depth of awareness in all experiences. We treasure awareness when we contact it in our interactions with other human intelligences. We use the limitations on the amount of awareness in other people's attitudes as an indication of the amount of past distress accumulated on, and temporarily interfering with the operation of, their intelligence.

25. Even though most cultures, societies, theoretical systems, and existing philosophies persistently deny the existence of freedom of viewpoint and freedom of choice, we, intuitively to begin with, and explicitly as we progress, claim and assert and seek to function on the basis of *complete* freedom of choice, of *complete* freedom of decision. If we have not and do not yet demonstrate this in practice, we assert that it is nevertheless our goal and that it can and will be reached with discharge, re-evaluation, and re-emergence.

26. Although existing societies, cultures, systems of thought, and repressive institutions deny the concept of total individual power, we assert its possession as part of our inherent natures. We systematically explore ways of reclaiming it. We view any up-until-the-moment restrictions or failures to utilize it fully as simply caused by patterns of past hurt which have not yet been sufficiently contradicted and discharged. We set the reclaiming of this inherent individual total power as our goal for ourselves and for all people. We reject the usual societal implication that reclaiming this individual power will lead to conflict between people, insisting that it will lead to mutual cooperative triumphs for all who approach it and to the degree that they attain it.

27. It is always better to cooperate than to compete.

28. There is no *real* conflict of interest between any two human intelligences or groups of human intelligences.

29. Any really good solution to a problem is a good solution for every human touched by that problem.

30. The inherent drive to survival through increasing the numbers of one's descendants, observable in all forms of life, is excellent and valuable but is not inherently compulsive. It can be brought under the domination of intelligence so that overpopulation by any one species of living things, including our own, need not threaten the survival, nor lead to the threatened extinction of, any other forms of life.

31. Interference with or manipulation of the environmental factors of our planet needs to be pursued or permitted only with the greatest and most thoughtful care for the results and only with the longest-range perspectives in mind.

32. Neatness, beauty, and order enhance the quality of life for all.

33. Goals should never be pursued that lead to any form of stasis but only goals that lead to fresh challenges and more interesting results.

34. All religious concepts arose as attempts to project a vision of a real, intuitively-sensed, human nature out of the confusion, the occluding lacks of knowledge, the perpetrated mistaken information, and the accumulated patterned nonsense and oppression in individual attitudes and in the social cultures that developed. The crucial characteristics of this human nature that are being reached for in these religious

concepts are exactly those of having no limits, needing no limits, accepting no limits, setting one's own program, following one's own will, continually achieving what had sometimes seemed impossible to achieve at previous stages.

35. We assume that it is possible to solve all of the problems of planet-wide human societies or national human societies. At our present state of experience we assume that this can be prepared for by experimenting, discussing, and revising the handling of problems within smaller groupings of people. It will be necessary that these groups of people have provided for good communication with each other, that no ideas or proposals are required to be "believed in" or treated as immune from challenge and question, and that every proposed solution to any problem is welcomed to be discussed and cautiously experimented with. It will be helpful in such discussions if agreement is reached with a long-standing RC assumption, that is, that *there is at least one elegant solution to any real problem.*

Such smaller groupings should never be restricted to, but should include, the Re-evaluation Counseling Communities as a possible useful smaller grouping.

The Reasons for the "No-Socializing" Principle in Co-Counseling

5.277 Co-Counselors are required, and expected, to refrain from setting up any additional, non-counseling relationships with a person whom they meet in the context of Co-Counseling, or in the Co-Counseling Community. This is because the Co-Counseling relationship, or co-participation in Co-Counseling activities, is such a precious and important relationship that it is crucially important to keep it "clean" and functional. As Co-Counselor, one hopes and expects to be assisted to re-emerge from all distress to one's own inherent, splendid nature and abilities, and one undertakes to assist others to do the same.

This does not mean that Co-Counselors will not become fond of each other or love each other. (They inevitably do.) It does mean that this precious commitment must not be diluted or contaminated by using the person for some other relationship, the purpose of which will inevitably turn out to be in conflict with the basic commitment towards Co-Counseling, and will carry, or soon acquire, some component of satisfying a patterned or "frozen" need.

Because people often begin counseling in a state of relative isolation and loneliness, and are starved for affection, and, as a result, have felt incompetent about setting up relationships

Reprinted from **The List**, Second Edition. Also appeared in **Present Time** No. 97, October 1994.

in the wide world, the presence of the Co-Counselor who is acting interested and validating towards one, often seems enormously attractive and inviting. It is easy for the person who is client to project on the counselor the longed-for satisfaction of all one's dreams of companionship, romance, love, business partnership, marriage, and any other close relationships.

It is very easy for people in the grip of such frozen "needs" or "yearnings" to deceive themselves. This phenomenon operates in the wide world ("when your heart's on fire, smoke gets in your eyes"), but people tend to be somewhat on guard in the usual wide-world situation where the very real attractiveness of the Co-Counseling relationship is not present to distort their thinking.

People who do not take the rules and warnings of the Co-Counseling *Guidelines* seriously in this respect are likely to create difficulties for themselves, for each other, and for their Co-Counseling associates in the Co-Counseling Community. It is difficult and confusing enough if only one Co-Counselor gets caught up in such feelings and dramatizations, but when two people turn such patterns on each other, the confusion is multiplied. They are likely to insist that it is their "own business." They will tell other people and Community leaders that as long as they are "two consenting adults" it "must be all right." However, if they do not refrain from these socializing relationships they will almost certainly "blame" Co-Counseling for "having caused the (inevitable) disaster."

This is why the Community makes it a *rule* that Co-Counselors do not "socialize." With progress and re-emergence it comes to be viewed as a necessary *principle* even though their conformity is now by informed agreement instead of an enforced requirement from the Community.

(Among the millions of people who have begun Co-Counseling to date, there are a certain number who could not resist their "feelings" and socialized with, went into business with, romanced, dated, or married Co-Counselors. Suffice it to say that *not one such relationship* has ever worked well no matter how enthusiastically the people's patterns began it nor what effort was expended in an attempt to make it workable. Inevitably the partners came to feel *betrayed* by each other because they had connived with each other's patterns and had abandoned the meaningful commitment that they had begun with of helping each other re-emerge and regain each person's full humanness.)

These feelings which come up (of being so attracted to one's Co-Counselor) are actually brought up by the person's basic intelligence as an opportunity for discharge, and if the person's counselor treats them as such, a great deal of progress can be made very quickly in important areas. It is quite all right to ask the leaders of the Community for help in getting such discharge started.

One hint: if the attracted person will sit about eight feet away from the person they are feeling attracted to and vehemently and repetitively voice every possible expression of the listening person's attractiveness in a voice dripping with emotion and yearning, discharge will tend to occur very quickly. If the attraction is mutual, the parties should take turns encouraging each other to great heights of exaggerated sentimentality. A couple of hours of laughter discharge each way is likely to convert the agonized pair into relaxed Co-Counselors, vastly relieved to have the air cleared of the frozen needs and the mawkish sentimentality that had threatened their valuable relationship.

Confused people have sometimes complained that a Co-Counseling relationship is not "real" because they are not encouraged to mess it up by adding patterned activities and strong feelings to it. The truth is that the Co-Counseling relationship is very "real." It is useful and rich because it is strongly and clearly defined. Someone has said it has the beauty of a poem or a song that uses a strict poetic form to achieve great complexity and communication.

The Co-Counseling Community and its teachers and leaders make a great effort to warn people of the importance of the no-socializing rule and principle (often called, in slang, the "blue pages" because of the color of paper with which it was originally added to the Co-Counseling *Manuals)*. People are warned and are told not to push socializing on other Co-Counselors whom they meet in classes or Community functions. They are not policed or spied upon (it is their "neck" and their happiness that is at risk). People may not, however, become teachers or leaders in the Re-evaluation Counseling Community if they persist in violating this principle that is part of the requirement of being a member. Be warned.

5.278 Keeping your relationships within the Re-evaluation Counseling Community "clean" (that is, rational) will lead you to discharge all the patterns which have ever given you trouble with any wide-world relationships as well.

People naturally, intuitively, and inherently seek and build excellent relationships with other humans. Where difficulties appear it must necessarily be where patterns, sometimes involving poor communication, have intruded. If the pattern is attached to the other person in the relationship, it becomes an interesting challenge to understand it and help the person discharge it. If the difficulty is more persistent than that, it implies that you, the first person in the relationship, have a pattern intruding from your side into the relationship and causing the difficulty as well. Tackle this possibility as a client in *your* session, and the difficulty will be resolved, often with surprising ease.

Money Matters and
Re-evaluation Counseling

Money and financial matters are often made to appear confusing and difficult to understand. It will be useful for us to see beyond this confusion and become able to deal with the underlying reality of financial affairs.

The reality is, even in this society, that money can be an easy, matter-of-fact part of living. We can enjoy taking care of our money and use it to enhance or facilitate our activities and goals, including our RC work, rather than having it be a difficulty or a hindrance.

Money need not be a nuisance. Being short of it is part of the functioning of the oppressive society, but handling money need not be difficult. We have done well at handling money matters in our Re-evaluation Counseling relationships. As we apply our theory and discharge our acquired distresses on the subject, any remaining problems can undoubtedly be solved.

This is aside, of course, from the basic oppression of *economic exploitation*, which most of us have a long-range goal of ending and replacing with a society where everyone has a job and everyone receives full value for his or her work. What I am talking about in this article is *managing* under *present* conditions.

Appeared in **Present Time** No. 97, October 1994.

What gets in the way? Well, distress, of course. All of us, without exception, have had a good deal of distress placed upon us about all aspects of money. We have been trained to distrust each other about money, to be competitive about it, to be reluctant to contribute money to any group projects where we do not immediately receive direct benefits back to us *individually*.

We have been cheated and exploited financially so many times that many of us, offended by others getting "something for nothing" at our expense, have slipped into the other end of the distress recording and are pulled by it to try to "get something for nothing" for ourselves in our dealings with each other. We have all been made to feel insecure about money. This was caused by financial hardship if our families were short of money. It was caused by fear of losing it and by feelings of guilt for having it, if our families *had* money.

This general anxiety about money, which is conditioned onto all individuals in this society, also acts to confuse us and to reinforce our powerlessness. Whenever we take some fresh initiative to improve our lives, by stepping out of the conformity patterns of the culture and doing something meaningful like Co-Counseling, or when we start to cooperate with each other in a meaningful project like the RC Community, anxiety about money is likely to be restimulated.

If we discharge and clear away these patterned attitudes, we will find that we "have all the money we need," that we can relaxedly pool enough contributions to achieve the joint projects we want, that we can receive a great deal of benefit and satisfaction back from what money we contribute to such joint projects.

Between us we have enough money—that we would be willing and able to use for RC purposes—to do everything we need to do, without hardship to anyone.

Miracles of money-raising have already been accomplished in the RC Communities. The Communities have never received any subsidies from outside, have always been completely financially independent, and yet have been able to finance rapid growth of Re-evaluation Counseling around the world. We have achieved great flexibility, freedom, and initiative in spending our funds. Though, of necessity, we have had to function within a profit-oriented society, we have nevertheless been able to handle and use money in a human way and for human purposes.

The agreements we have already reached between us on the collection and use of our money are simple, workable, and understandable. Only distress attached to money makes anyone feel confused about those agreements.

Basically, everyone in RC contributes to the financial support of our Communities and activities. Our goal is that everyone contributes freely and without hardship and in proportion to their ability to contribute. We have another goal, which we have not been able to realize fully yet, of no person ever being barred from Re-evaluation Counseling activities for financial reasons. We have moved toward this goal with the use of scholarships, subsidies, literature contributions, and a great deal of volunteer work.

The Communities ask everyone who participates in classes, workshops, or other Community activities, to contribute their share to the financial expenses of such activities. Every class and workshop is also intended to be a place for the collection of additional "outreach" funds, which can be used for scholarships and subsidies for later workshops and classes, for individuals who would otherwise find it difficult to attend. These "outreach" subsidies and scholarships have by no means eliminated differences in the financial difficulties of various people participating, but they have often made it *possible* for people to participate who would not otherwise have been able to do so. They are a step in the right direction. They have helped as much as we have been able to afford financially under our existing level of clarity and organization.

Teachers of RC classes and leaders of RC workshops are free to set the fees for these activities, hopefully with a good balance between the potential participants' ability to pay and the need of the teacher and the Community and its various functions to be financed. Thus, any RC teacher is free to set the fee for her or his classes and to vary it for any student. Currently all RC teachers are urged to offer five *free* places in any class they teach, three for young people (who have great difficulty in getting their hands on money for these purposes) and two for Third World people or people of color (who suffer such acute financial discrimination in the present white-dominated societies that financial assistance in getting started in RC will often make the decisive difference as to whether they attempt it or not).

Almost all the work done for the RC Communities is unpaid. The only notable exceptions are the RC teachers, who are allowed as individual enterprisers to charge for their classes, and workshop leaders, who charge a fee for leading a workshop. This fits well with the conditioning of the society that "you pay for everything you get" or "you get what you pay for." It takes advantage of people's expectation that they will have to pay for any service they receive.

By Community agreement (the *Guidelines*), all class fees are planned so that one-fourth of the total amount paid does not go to the teacher at all, not even for the expenses of the class, but goes directly into the "Outreach" Funds of the Community. These are used to pay for scholarships and subsidies and to interest and support new populations in becoming involved in Re-evaluation Counseling.

In the case of workshops, a 10% fee for the use of the Re-evaluation Counseling name is figured into the cost of the workshop and sent to the Community Service Fund of Personal Counselors for servicing the activities of the Re-evaluation Counseling Communities. In addition, any surplus income above the expenses of the workshop (which include the basic fees agreed upon for the leader and the organizer) is used similarly. For International and Regional workshops, the surplus income is divided four ways, with one-twelfth going to the organizer (for the extra work of handling a bigger workshop), one-fourth to the leader (for the extra work of the leader), one-third to the International Outreach Fund, and one-third to the Publications Fund of Rational Island Publishers to subsidize publication of Re-evaluation Counseling literature, which could not be published without such a subsidy. For local or Area workshops, any surplus income is divided, three-quarters to the Area Outreach Fund and one-quarter to the leader of the workshop.

The money collected for Outreach from Area workshops or from classes is again divided, with seven-tenths of it being at the disposal of the local Community for doing Outreach to populations under-represented in their Community and three-tenths being turned over to the International Outreach Fund to support reaching and involving people in new national, ethnic, or geographical populations, with different languages, etc.

(At the World Conference of the RC Communities in November of 1993, the *Guidelines* were modified to say that "these [Outreach] funds may also be used for the purpose of equalizing to some extent the opportunities available to people whose inherent situations make it necessary to have assistance for full participation in Re-evaluation Counseling activities.")

The portions of the *Guidelines* of the International RC Communities that refer to finances are simple, clear, and easily understandable.

Ours is an effective system. It has allowed large numbers of people to sample Co-Counseling at a class or workshop who could not have been reached otherwise. It has allowed many local Communities to build some "Outreach" financial reserves for later expansion. It has enabled the International Community to grow across oceans, continents, language barriers, and national boundaries, and to establish the beginnings of excellent Communities in seventy-seven different countries in a relatively short period of time.

Since there is so much that RCers and the RC Community would like to do, so much of the world population yet to be reached, there is never "enough" Outreach money. Having our goals ahead of our current capabilities is probably a permanent condition but also a healthy one.

The Re-evaluation Foundation, completely independent of the Communities, undertakes to raise additional money from contributions of various sorts and to initiate or support certain special projects across cultural, language, and national barriers. As more skill, experience, and attention can be directed to these fund-raising activities, they may become a significant factor in the financial support of the growth of RC. (Until now the Outreach Funds have been the principal financial life-blood of the Communities.)

Some Communities have set up "maintenance" funds in various ways to pay for routine expenses that cannot properly be classed as outreach to new populations. In the past, these expenses were often met from the Outreach Funds, but as the Communities have become more stable and better organized, there is everywhere a desire to reserve Outreach Funds for actual outreach to new populations and to take care of other financial needs by raising money for them as they occur.

A fairly recent but hopeful development in the Re-evaluation Counseling Communities has been using counseling itself on the distress and confusion associated with money. Support groups about finances are being organized at many workshops. The reports are that discharge is easily available on these topics and that the results are beneficial in many areas of one's life. With discharge, the topic of money seems to lose much of its ability to confuse the client. He or she becomes more able to handle money, including financial contributions to RC, relaxedly and with ease.

The benefits of counseling on money seem to reach far beyond the topic itself. It has been reported by a number of people that "counseling on money is like counseling on sex. You discharge in the one area but the results affect every area of your life."

We need Co-Counselors to become "money experts" who are able to think clearly in this area. We need people who can come up with good, sensible, economical ways of raising necessary funds. We need people who can organize this activity so well that our Communities are well-financed, that no member suffers financial hardship to attend RC activities, and that adequate access to RC is available to new Co-Counselors without regard to their economic circumstances.

1981, revised 1994

Realistic Planning
in the Present

The Present Situation for
Working-Class People

Sometime, probably not later than nine and not earlier than eighteen billion years ago, the universe began. It began with a "big bang" explosion of a very condensed, very small entity. It exploded either into space around it or it created the space around it in the process of exploding. The energy and matter released in this "big bang" have continued to expand since that time and have taken many forms. Matter and energy have assembled in this expanding universe into galaxies, stars, planets, dust clouds, and radiation of many different kinds. Whole galaxies have assembled, collided, and pressure-cooked new forms of matter, and much matter has at least partially disappeared into "black holes," whose ultimate fate and disposal has so far only been guessed at.

Planets developed around at least some stars and possibly around most stars. The star with which we are most familiar, our sun, became surrounded by nine planets and a wealth of smaller bodies—asteroids, comets, meteorites, gas, etc. The conditions on one planet, our own Earth, happened to be such that complicated chemical reactions could take place. Out of these reactions developed entities of increasing complexity which were increasingly independent of the surroundings. Some of these entities became self-replicating.

Appeared in **Present Time** No. 92, July 1993.

This is the basic characteristic of life. Over a long period of time these living entities evolved into more and more complex living relationships. These earliest forms of life developed more than three and a half billion years ago. The planet itself has been in existence for perhaps six billion years.

These self-replicating ("living") entities continued to increase in complexity through the process of evolution. Over long spans of time more and more complex forms of life evolved. (This evolution continued in spite of occasional great annihilations of life due to meteorite or comet impacts upon the earth.) At some point, estimated at about one million years ago, some forms of life developed the ability to be intelligent, to do what we now call "thinking." This can be understood as responding to an environmental situation, not with a rigid, pre-set response as all living organisms previously had done, but with a new successful response to each new situation which the creature confronted. (These creatures were humans, of our own species, or perhaps of closely related species which have since become extinct.)

These humans developed languages and other forms of communication. They began to create and use tools. They increasingly mastered the environment with these and other inventions. They gradually spread into nearly all habitable parts of the earth and developed a rich genetic pool in the variances which the different environments encouraged. They all remained very closely related, however, and at present all humans everywhere upon the earth are members of the same sub-species. What did evolve, rapidly, however, was their cultures. As these humans developed languages and used their vast, accurate memories, cultural, art, and written information passed on more and more accumulated knowledge from one generation to another.

THE VULNERABILITY TO DISTRESS PATTERNS

This flexible intelligence of humans was vulnerable from the beginning to the imposition of distress patterns. These distress patterns were, in effect, setbacks to a more primitive type of functioning. They were imposed whenever the (apparently somewhat delicate) thinking ability was interrupted by a distressing or painful situation. Under these conditions the incoming information is stored in a rigid form by the human, rather than in the flexible, easily available form in which information from non-distressing situations is filed. This kind of rigid storage may be currently observed occurring in other mammals. It operates as a kind of crude "learning" for these other mammals in which the inherited, rigid, instinctive behavior is replaced by a new rigid behavior pattern which may actually represent a better adjustment to an environmental factor than was the instinctive behavior which it replaced.

With humans, the operation of this mechanism sharply and steeply degrades the functioning of the human from intelligent, mastering flexibility to sub-human, rigid reactions. It leaves a residue of rigid, non-thinking, inflexible behavior which can be triggered by a similar situation in the future. (It can also be triggered by the human's attempt to explore the puzzling residue left by the distress.) Then it once again takes over, degrades the total functioning, and adds new effect and scope to the area of misfunctioning.

There is an apparently built-in *drive* or *motivation* to remove these rigidities with certain processes that are available to the human, but which do not operate well or thoroughly, except during aware cooperation between at least two intelligences. These processes can easily become interfered with and made nearly unavailable through the operation of other distresses.

In the early ages of human existence distress patterns were acquired and accumulated through accidental mishaps or through the "contagion" of being hurt by someone else's distress recording. Each generation had a fairly good chance of "starting over" with a clean slate.

When humans' mastery of the environment reached the point that one individual could produce or accumulate more than the wherewithal which would support himself or herself and family (typically, but not always, through the development of agriculture or animal husbandry) the stage was set for greater domination of human affairs by distress patterns. Greed and violence patterns undoubtedly already existed, accumulated and preserved through happenstance interactions between humans. Now the possibility of "wealth" could be speculated about. The production of one person, now possible beyond that one person's survival needs, could be taken from that person by force. That person could then be forced to keep creating additional wealth for the exploiter. War captives need no longer be killed or adopted into the tribe but could be kept in servitude with threats, propaganda, and the installation of submissive patterns, for the enrichment of their captors. The first class society had begun.

These first class societies are always slaveowner-slave societies. They appeared for a while to "work," in that the environment was exploited more effectively because of the organization accompanying the exploitation. Populations grew much larger than before. City-states were organized. Resources were devoted to intellectual activity, often in the guise of religious practices.

The period of slaveowner-slave societies lasted roughly four thousand years overall. Certain built-in unworkabilities or "contradictions" eventually led to the collapse of the slave societies and their replacement by feudal societies, in which the principal classes were feudal lords or *barons* and *serfs*. The serfs were not owned outright by the barons as the slaves had been by the slave owners, but were almost as totally dominated by them.

The feudal societies have tended to endure between one and two thousand years before certain unworkabilities, backed by the basic human resistance to oppression, brought about *their* replacement by the current form of class society.

The current owning-class-working-class societies are about 350 to 400 years old. They have allowed and exploited an enormous increase in the productivity of human labor. They have permitted, tolerated, and in some ways encouraged an enormous increase in the total amount of human knowledge about the universe, the planet, life, and the details of human existence, *provided only* that certain falsehoods, which are supportive of oppression, are never allowed to be seriously exposed or challenged.

THE "MIDDLE" CLASSES

In all three forms of the oppressive societies, a portion of the oppressed class has been assigned a special role. This is to act as the agent of the oppressors in managing, organizing, and improving the efficiency of the exploitation of the rest of the oppressed class. In the slave societies, these were privileged slaves, overseers, scribes, artists, and so on. In the feudal societies, the overseers, guild masters, scribes, clergy, knights, and intellectuals were the "middle" class. The current middle class includes intellectuals, technicians, managers, professors, religious figures, professionals of all sorts, and factory superintendents.

In our present society these "middle classes" are fundamentally part of the working class. They produce much more value than they receive as salaries and perks, just as the regular working-class people produce far more value than they receive as wages and fringe benefits. However, the patterns installed upon these "middle-class" people in the process of their conditioning in childhood and youth tend to be distinctly different than the patterns which have been installed upon those of us who "know we are working class."

For liberation purposes, it has worked best to treat the people conditioned to think they are "middle class" as part of the working classes, while remembering that it is *necessary to win them* as dependable allies for the working class as a whole. They can be won by understanding their patterns, helping them to become free of them, treating them as individuals as "agents of the working class within the middle class," and welcoming them back to the working class as their patterns are discharged and their clarity increases.

THE OWNING CLASS

It also works best to take a similar attitude to members of the *owning class*. It is one of the great strengths of RC theory that we can realize that all of us, from all classes, from all different cultural backgrounds, are basically just alike in our fundamental characteristics. It is best that we remember that individuals in the working class, in the middle class, and the owning class are fundamentally just the same, but that each of us has been victimized by the class oppression into different ways of being miserable. If we remember this and act on it, we can convert these owning-class people, who have supposedly been committed by their conditioning to our oppression and exploitation, into firm, effective, human allies for the complete liberation of the working class. This means the liberation of humanity.

If confident working-class people say to owning-class people, "You are our children, who were stolen from us in your infancy and placed under vicious "enchantments" which have spoiled the humanness of your lives and used you against us, against all your human instincts," the owning-class people are often moved to heavy grief discharge. If we further say to them, "We welcome you back to the working class and will help you discharge these vicious enchantments (patterns) that have been placed upon you," we open the possibility of having very useful and effective allies in contact with us from now on.

WE WORKING-CLASS PEOPLE

We working class are almost the entire population of the world, even in technically advanced countries such as the United States, England, Germany, and Japan. We constitute close to 90% of the population there, and our numbers are even greater in countries with less advanced technologies. Part of us, of course, at least think we are "middle-class" (until we notice that the economic depression forces us into unemployment just about as fast as it does the wage workers).

We working-class people are the humanity of the future. Societies divided into classes are no longer workable. They are collapsing in almost every aspect of their functioning. They are still producing billionaires at an accelerating rate but they are also producing starving and homeless populations at an even greater rate. They are cooperating to keep small "wars" in progress on the basis of long out-of-date nationalisms, "religious differences," and ridiculous claims that security lies in production of more arms. These class societies are facing populations, however, which have shown they will no longer tolerate world wars. They are facing populations to whom the debris left by several generations of Cold War activities is now plainly visible as a long-term fraudulent manipulation of the world's people.

The existing class societies are no longer able to keep people terrified and unthinking through the threat of general nuclear holocaust, as they did for so many years. The oppressive class societies can at present seem to only repeat the less and less believable inanities of past propagandas.

The collapsing class societies can, perhaps, for a while longer, go on piling up larger accumulations of the valuable capital produced by the workers of the past and the present which was looted from them and is still being looted from them at the present. The collapsing class societies have, up to now, been able to manipulate the populations during most elections. They have been able until now to see that the voters are only offered choices between such stark right-wing dodo candidates like Bush and Major, and pretentious "liberals" such as Clinton or the "Labor Party" heads in England. When such "liberals" are allowed to win elections, they are never allowed by the real masters of the economy (who paid for their elections) to do more than demonstrate their own lack of courage, lack of real principles, and general ineptitude. This, of course, is intended to conveniently pave the way for the return of the right-wing dodos in the next farcical election.

WHAT CAN WE DO?

Can the working class simply wait for the oppressive society to collapse of its own contradictions? I think it would be most unwise of us to do so. Enormous suffering by the finest people and the most innocent people in the world could take place while we waited.

It has taken hundreds of millions of years for the tremendous, precious variety of living things we share the planet with to evolve, yet most of them are in danger of being wiped out in a few years by the blind rapacity of the oppressive society's system of profiteering exploitation.

The oceans, the lakes and streams, the atmosphere, the soil, the forests, all can be ruined if we allow the present society to stagger on. If we continue to operate within the patterns which have been placed upon us, we give free reign to the patterns which have been placed upon the owning class.

Our lives are demeaned and distorted by timidity, submissiveness, tolerance of alcohol and drugs, willingness to be distracted by "shopping," sports loyalties and enthusiasms, and sensational journalism. "Religious" pronouncements and "patriotic" appeals will be used to distract us from our clear responsibility as the great majority of the population of our planet to *take charge of things* and see that intelligence operates in human affairs.

Is it possible for humans to have a decent society, one without exploitation? I think it is possible, beyond question.

Great steps toward such a society were attained briefly in the Paris Commune in 1879, and for a much longer time in the early years of the Soviet Republics. Very profound progress towards such a society was achieved in liberated China as long as Mao Tse Tung was alive and his influence determined policy for China. Thousands of years of famines in China were brought to an end, probably permanently, and much until-then wasteland was bent to a supportive role for humans, with great labor but also with great success. In the Soviet Union illiteracy was wiped out, health resources were made available universally, a backward economy was brought to modernity, everyone had a job, great advances were made in math and science. This was achieved in spite of repeated mass invasions from other countries, isolation from other societies, and enormous losses suffered of life and capital.

Is socialism working now in the former Soviet countries? Is it working now in China? No. It is not. It is not working, but not because socialism is not "workable." It is not working because the patterns of the oppressive society persisted and found roots in the minds of the leadership in both countries and led to the re-establishment of an owning-class-working-class society in disguise. This society still claimed to be a socialist or communist society, but it actually reverted to an owning-class-working-class society in which communist party leaders played the role of owning-class exploiters.

I do not think there is any question that intelligent people can make a non-exploitative society work, and work extremely well. I suspect at this point, however, that "socialist" principles will not be enough. I suspect we're going to have to have the tools of RC working right along with the principles of socialism.

THE ROLE OF RCERS

What will be special in the role of working-class RCers, at least at first, that is different than the role of any working-class person?

First and foremost, *we do know how to be smarter tomorrow than we were yesterday.* We know how to use counseling to discharge old blocks on our thinking and we know how to use counseling to review and improve our thinking day by day. Any situation about the universe, the world, the human race, the working class, our close associates, or ourselves that needs to be thought well about will be thought about better if we first take turns listening to each other think out loud about it.

We know that in such discussions, and in any discussions in fact that ever take place anywhere, the thinking will be greatly enhanced by securing agreement that no one speaks twice before everyone has spoken once, and that no one speaks four times before everyone has spoken twice. It's a simple principle, but it works.

We know that people are basically good, no matter how badly they have been acting. We know that people want to be reached and brought into agreement no matter how different the appearance is which they give. We know some of the skills that we can use to help them achieve this.

We know that all people are intelligent if we can reach through their patterns. We know that people who are pretentious and dogmatic about "having all the answers" do not, in general, know any more than we do. We know that we do not need to give in to anything which we are not satisfied is correct.

GETTING ORGANIZED

We know that having a correct policy by itself is not enough. We know that organization of people is necessary. We know that action must follow correct policy and good organization if either of them is to have meaning. We know that everyone would like to be a leader. We know that solving any shortage of leadership simply requires encouraging people to become leaders.

We know there is no real conflict of interest between people in different groups, between people who were born into or forced into different classes, between people of different genders, languages, skin colors, attitudes. We know that working-class people of all nations have a common interest in supporting each other to end each other's oppression by the societies and owning-class structures in the individual nations. We know that all organizations need to establish and maintain connections with working-class people in other nations.

We know that labor union organization is crucial and central, but we also know that the old type of labor organization is not enough. We need organizations of women. We need support groups and leaders' groups for men, for women, for young people of all ages, for older people of all ages. We need "clubs," support groups, or caucuses for every language group, every national group in every neighborhood, every city, every factory. If we set up groups where people listen to each other, they *will* evolve good programs. We need groups for the unemployed, groups for office workers, groups for food workers. We need political organizations that will sponsor candidates and use election campaigns for educational publicity in every election. We need to build coalitions between our working-class groups and middle-class and even owning-class groups (owning-class women, for example, can readily become firm allies on issues involving children, the environment, etc.).

We need to work out our individual goals but also our goals for our families, our friends, our groups, and for the working class. When we have clear goals for the working class, we can establish clear goals for all humanity.

Is there any real conflict between our own individual goals, those of the working class, and those of humanity as a whole? Not if we are rational in our thinking about them.

Do we need to be in support groups? Yes, otherwise the restimulation of daily living is likely to creep up on us. Do we need regular sessions? Yes, otherwise we will slip into living a low-quality life as the pulls of old patterns take over and drown our days in senseless patterned routines. Do we need occasional Wygelian leaders' meetings? Yes, or we will lose the perspective of being in charge of our lives and activities. Do we need to act as leaders and encourage other people into leadership? Yes, otherwise a vital element of correct functioning will be missing.

Can we do it?

Of course we can.

General Agreements to Guide
a Future Society

In spite of our sometimes being preoccupied with our day-to-day survival in this collapsing society and in spite of any tendency to emphasize our re-emergence from distress, many RCers are interested in thinking about what a non-oppressive society of the future can be like, not just in its philosophy, but in its operation.

Is it possible to stop the destruction of the environment quickly enough? Is it possible to totally eliminate the senseless wars that are still persisting in some localities? Can we plan a decent society and describe it in a way that will inspire enthusiasm and hope among the disillusioned and confused?

Speculating about such a future society has been for a long time one of my favorite musings. Possibly it's time to share this activity more widely and see what kind of tentative blueprints might grow out of our thinking after a few months of discussion.

Below are some of my thoughts that I can remember easily. What do you think of them? What do you object to? What further ideas immediately spring to your mind?

—Harvey Jackins

1. Nothing shall be used from the environment without taking complete responsibility to see that it is returned to the

Appeared in **Present Time** No. 88, July 1992.

environment intact or reintroduced into an operating recovery cycle in ways that will not interfere with the operation of the forms of life involved. This includes air, water, mineral resources, the soil, and the harvesting of all forms of life including forests and sea life.

2. The surface of the earth will be largely reserved for the support and livability of other forms of life. We will view ourselves as respectful guests and visitors as well as benign caretakers and supporters of the web of life around us. Human dwellings, human transportation routes, and human manufacturing activities shall be in the main located underground, deep enough not to interfere with the activities of other forms of life on the surface of the earth.

3. All extinguished forms of life, whenever possible, shall be reconstituted through the application of genetic engineering. All presently surviving as well as reconstituted forms of life shall be deemed sacred and shall be preserved. Forms of life harmful to, parasitic upon, or predatory toward human beings (smallpox virus, HIV, malarial parasites, etc.) shall be removed from the general environment and kept only in carefully guarded containers in the most responsible laboratory conditions. Threatening kinds of mosquitoes, tsetse flies, ticks, lice, etc., shall be genetically modified to prevent their harassing of humans or their filling their previous roles as vectors for the transmission of disease organisms. In all other possible ways humans shall be protected from assault by traditionally competing organisms or organisms predatory toward humans. However, no strain of organism shall be wiped out. Each will be viewed as an incomparably precious resource.

4. A network of aquifers shall be tunneled several hundred feet under the surface of all existing continents and supplied

with fresh water from the ice caps of Greenland and Antarctica. This will be made available for the intelligent support and modification of the climate and vegetation, and for the growing of desirable crops.

5. No human being shall be deemed in any way inferior to or superior to any other human being.

6. No human being shall be required to conform to any standards simply for the sake of conformity. Cooperation shall be secured by communication, and enforcement shall never be used except as a temporary emergency measure.

7. A minimum standard of living shall be established. No advances in the standard of living of other people shall take place until everyone is functioning at or above the minimum standard.

This will include the support, special equipment, and dedicated helpers necessary for disabled, disadvantaged, and uneducated people to function at this minimum standard of living.

Somewhat higher standards of living shall be established on not more than two levels slightly above the minimum standard. Barriers to the passage of individuals from the lower levels to the next higher levels shall be systematically ameliorated.

Once the three levels of living standards have been set and are in operation, the standards may be improved, but only if the lower standards improve at the same rate as the higher.

Special recognition and reward may be granted to outstanding individuals by the society as a whole, but only after full publicity and discussion and a vote by the entire population approving such recognition and reward.

8. Over-population shall be prevented by requiring would-be parents to qualify and receive permission to conceive a child after having thoroughly reviewed and discharged the distresses of their own childhoods, and after having worked as helpers in the care and education of children under expert and respected supervision. Such parents must have qualified as "assistant parents" and must present a program of pledged contacts with other parents or qualified candidates for parenting to provide collective contact between the children and the families. This will be organized to eliminate the possibility of isolation or loneliness for the children. Big families used to provide such resource, but they will not be available in the small family future. Small families will be necessary for a stable population of humans which will not crowd, threaten, or extinguish the functioning of other species of life.

9. Expansion of humanity *through the universe* shall become an accepted goal and be planned and organized for. The momentum of the growth in population already underway will be handled temporarily by the construction of great floating continents in the climactically favorable portions of the Pacific Ocean. More long-range projects will allow the terraforming of the moon, the modification of Mars and Venus to make them habitable, and the development of the technology for reaching and colonizing other star systems.

10. All past knowledge shall be catalogued, stored, and made available, using the rapidly advancing skills and capacity of computer technology, and all new information as it appears shall be automatically added to the existing store. Access to any and all such information shall be available to every human as the privilege and right of being human.

There will be no "secret" knowledge. Creating and servicing this world-wide library will be a principal responsibility of the world government which will necessarily come into being.

11. Complete democracy will become possible by possession by each human of a television-like device where information about any subject, including public affairs, is available by keying a request into the instrument. Where decisions need to be made that affect groups of people, those groups will be notified of the information available on the relevant subjects and will be urged to watch presentations of such information on their instrument. Once all points of view have been presented, debates and discussions will be scheduled. When people are well-informed, a vote (which may be as large as world-wide in scope), will be taken by people inserting their unique personal keys into their unique personal instruments and voting yes or no on the crucial question. The results will be tabulated and appear on their screen almost immediately, in the case of local issues, but within a day or so even on world-wide issues.

12. The surface of the earth will be largely reserved for the use of the forms of life which require sunlight, fresh air, etc. Some of these will be raised as crops, probably mostly in huge greenhouses (field-size), where insects and other forms of life which prey upon and attack the crops will be excluded rather than destroyed with poisons, insecticides, or herbicides.

Underground railroads will come close to the surface *at stations* but *travel* at a much lower level. Thus gravity will furnish the large amount of energy necessary for acceleration to running speed as well as the braking force which will slow the trains down in preparation for a stop at the next station. The trains will be driven by compressed air blowing them at running speeds, and computer-managed fans will exhaust the air in front of and compress it behind the traveling train. Such trains will travel on a roadbed in the inner one of two concentric tubes which floats on water partially filling the outer tube. Passenger travel on such trains can be very, very fast and very comfortable, far more comfortable than present planes. (Full-scale plans and engineering drawings are already in existence for the construction of such future railroads.)

13. Most present systems of levees on rivers will be replaced by the dredging of the river bottoms and the depositing of the rich soil on adjacent farmland so that the river can stay in its bed.

14. The great store of nutritious chemicals accumulated at the bottom of many oceans (which fortuitously, through natural upwelling, provide the rich fisheries on the west coast of South America and other places) will be brought to the surface in many other places as well so that our predation and use of sea life for our purposes will no longer threaten the supply of nutrients for other forms of life. The bringing of this rich bottom water to the surface, where its combination with the sunlight will produce an enormous increase in the fertility of the oceans, can be handled by low pressure steam turbines that use the difference in the energy levels of the cold bottom water and the warm surface water to pump the bottom water to the surface.

15. With the end of oppression and exploitation and the full development of computerized controls and robotics, it will become possible for people to "work with their hands" a maximum of a few hours a day to produce all the goods which we will find useful. In general, all people will participate in such "manual" labor to some degree. The children

will be educated to expect that they will also perform technical tasks, challenging intellectual work, and creative art. If people wish to work more in one field than another, permission will be granted by their fellow workers, because individual satisfactions will vary greatly in an atmosphere of freedom.

Those are a few of my favorite proposals. What thoughts do you have to contribute?

The Rational Role of Organizing

We have surmised that the role towards which humans must inevitably tend is that of observing, understanding, guiding, and enhancing the development of the universe around them towards greater survivability for themselves and for entities which are allied to them.

The universe will continue to function, will continue to change, quite without our intervention or permission, of course. Part of its changes (measured quantitatively, quite a lot of its changes), will be in a "downward trend" direction. Entropy will increase, at least in the processes about which we are well-informed. Galaxies will smash into each other in great conflagrations. "Black holes" will gobble up far-flung complexities and consign them to a not-as-yet well-imagined uniformity.

Yet increasing complexity will certainly be a characteristic of much of the activity of the universe. In the physical and intellectual arenas which we take and will take an interest in, our busy fingers, instruments, and minds will be initiating, enhancing, and enjoying *new* concepts. Excellent poetry, music, and other art will be created. Delightful vegetation will develop (more and more with our encouragement and benign intervention). A tremendous variety of animal life will emerge on our planet and on, possibly, hundreds of other planets. Some of these other living things will be moving closer and closer to the complexity which will permit intelligence to develop and function. We will someday be communicating with, and in joint action with, minds which will challenge us and open doors to viewpoints unattainable by our species alone.

We will be fully occupied for a long time to come with the care and enhancing of relatively small segments of this vast universe around us. We will be reaching to fill our glimpsed role of benign caretakers and enhancers of reality. We will be guiding the great communities of humans embedded in the greater communities of living things, thoroughly enjoying our role of caretakers and improvers of the planet or planets of our tenancy.

We will be occupied in emerging as expeditiously as possible from the turmoil and confusion of the past. This confusion was engendered by the activity of past humans struggling under the competing directions of their brilliant intelligences and the senseless, rigid patterns with which they had become victimized. These patterns had come about through accidental mishap, through the contagion of one patterned person imposing patterns on other individuals by hurting them, and, in the last six thousand years or so, by systematic imposition from the oppressive societies we had fallen into and remained captive to.

In the struggle to "re-emerge" into our potential brilliance and goodness, we have many areas of activity facing us.

One of these areas is individual re-emergence—the shedding of the patterns which have become attached to and parasitic upon our individual minds. Here our progress is accelerating as the number of deliberate re-emergers increases and their techniques improve.

Another area is precisely the increasing of our numbers by enlisting more intelligences and more viewpoints in the communication and sharing of our discoveries.

A third area is the interruption of the systematic imposition of patterns by the oppressive societies. This will lead to the eventual dismantling of the societies themselves and the replacement of them by societies functioning on rational thinking and on rational relationships.

To accomplish these ends we bring our abilities to think, to be aware, to freely choose our viewpoints and our paths of action. We bring our little-used-as-yet capacity for complete power of the individual as well as the great power of multiple intelligences acting in communication with each other. To these tasks we bring our evolving theory, the growing results of the thinking and communication between us in the past.

No matter how brilliantly and accurately we think, however, no matter how correctly and far-sightedly we plan, all will eventually be frustrated and wasted unless we *act*. Action requires *decision* by at least an individual. For action by more than a single individual, we need *organization*.

Humans have a long history of trying to organize for mutual goals, whether the goals were intelligent, destructive, or confused. Bands, teams, companies, congregations, armies, political parties, and societies have "organized." As individuals we have been "organized" in some manner all of our lives.

When we begin to consider organizing for rational purposes, we are faced with a vast variety of models already in existence in the society. We will probably be tempted to choose from among these for the beginnings of our own organizational forms.

After forty-four years of existence, Re-evaluation Counseling has evolved a variety of organizational forms of its own. We have a "Community." We have Regions, Areas, support groups, classes, workshops, conferences, Wygelian leaders' groups, discussion groups, caucuses, and commissions. Most of us probably take it for granted that these will serve us as we prepare to take action towards some new goal or more advanced cause.

We have leadership roles assigned and waiting to be assigned (and sometimes even well-defined), such as "Reference Person" (on three different levels), "Alternate Reference Person" (on two different levels), Re-evaluation Counseling Teacher, assistant Re-evaluation Counseling Teacher, workshop leader, workshop organizer, editor, translator, translation coordinator, etc., etc.

Which parts of this organizing have we done well? Where have we introduced rational principles of organization to replace the irrational, unworkable habits of organization in the oppressive society?

One rational initiative we have taken is the introduction of the practice of *trusting of leaders to make routine decisions without supervision by the membership* over extended periods of time. We have done well by proposing, and sometimes requiring, that *every person in a meeting speak once before any person speaks twice* (and that every person speak *twice* before any person speaks *four* times). This step has eliminated many of the usual barriers to effective discussions.

We have successfully organized innumerable varieties of workshops, conferences, support groups, and classes.

We have published a great variety of particular journals for groups of people who share certain special interests. (We have also published general journals for people on different levels of responsibility.) We have created, translated, and published many books, pamphlets, audio and video cassettes. We have published ninety-six issues of *Present Time*.

We have improved communication among us by grasping and using new developments in communication technology (long-distance telephoning, rapid mail, e-mail, facsimile, and conference calls).

We are still affected to a degree by the stasis modelled and imposed by the surrounding society. Here there is a need for immediate work to be done. An organization whose goal and purpose is to change and grow and achieve changes in the surroundings cannot be satisfied with "stability." *Growth* and *continual growth* must be a high priority for an organization such as ours. We have agreed upon this as a goal in the past, but usually without sufficient emphasis. I now emphasize it again, strongly.

One characteristic of our functioning has not been well-faced or dealt with. Perhaps we have now achieved enough success that we can face this. *Almost all of the growth in which we have taken such pride has been achieved by the initiatives, the efforts, and the persistence of a small portion of the numbers of people who are Co-Counseling.* The rest of us have been inhibited by our fears, embarrassments, or other distresses (or perhaps lured by the "comfort" of having things "stable") into comparative inactivity. To be satisfied with a lack of growth, a lack of change, with the "ease" of not having to deal with new situations, to be pleased with not having to "think," is an *addiction*. It is the conditioning of the past which has left us susceptible to this.

Often in the past when we have evolved successful new forms of organization, we have been careless about remembering to use them. We often reverted to old organizational forms that produced stasis because they were the "way we did things" in the past and were therefore festooned with patterns. Our splendid *Guidelines*, very carefully put together out of much actual experience, have often been at least partially ignored.

Experienced RCers often declare their great pleasure in having new people coming in to RC to share our concepts and become our co-workers within the RC Community. We have treasured and publicized examples of individuals who have boldly and openly offered RC knowledge to the people around them (and found these people eager to learn more of it and to use it). However, in practice, a large number of RCers still act as if RC were "too difficult" for anyone else to understand, and as if it were "too embarrassing" for us to tell other people about this precious knowledge.

No organization is functioning well unless it is *growing*. Perpetual growth is a sign of a healthy organization.

Every member of the organization should have been told that he or she is expected to move into leadership as quickly as she or he is able and willing to take the step. This expectation on each member of moving to a higher level of responsibility and leadership should be persistent.

Leadership should not cause financial hardship to a leader, but financial remuneration to the leader should not go beyond the standards for a working-class journeyman mechanic in the field. Middle-class or owning-class financial expectations should *not* be a standard for leading RC activities.

Outreach in the RC Communities is the investment of Community funds in extending an opportunity to new people to participate in RC activity. This assistance is intended to afford such people an opportunity to decide if they are interested in continuing to participate. It is an *investment* by the Community and is not, in general, a continuing subsidy.

Sharing, by providing financial assistance to low-income sections of the Community (such as the very young, the young, teen-agers, disabled people, unemployed people, elderly people, etc.), should be geared to the level of assistance that would be offered within a well-functioning "extended family" in the existing society, *if the Community's finances permit.* Contributions to such a "sharing" activity from Outreach Funds (of the Area Community or International Community) should be invited (or even suggested) to Community members of owning-class and middle-class status (but should never be imposed or enforced; all participation in RC must be free-will and from individual conviction) as contributions to assist in the transformation of the society to a classless one.

"Criticisms" of leaders should be directed personally by the individual with the criticism to the individual leader being criticized, and this should be done privately, by mail, phone, or in person. The issue should be discussed with the individual leader *before* it is discussed with anyone else. If the person with the criticism is still unsatisfied, he or she should then contact the leader responsible for that person in the RC structure. (Criticism of a class member or assistant teacher [once it has been taken up privately with the person criticized] should be taken up privately with the teacher of the class. Criticism of a teacher or Alternate Reference Person of an Area should be taken up with the Area Reference Person. Criticism of an Area Reference Person should be taken up with a Regional Reference Person. Criticism of a Regional Reference Person should be taken up with an International Reference Person or Alternate International Reference Person. Criticism of the International Reference Person or an

Alternate International Reference Person should be taken up with the other member of the duo.) If the criticizing person is not satisfied at this point, the last person appealed to should be asked to arrange a discussion with a peer group of the leader who is being criticized *and* the leader himself or herself. If this does not resolve the criticism, the person criticizing should resign from Re-evaluation Counseling.

The Palestine-Israel Agreement:
Just a Start,
But a Real Start, a Good Start

The Re-evaluation Counseling Communities, world-wide, enthusiastically congratulate all Palestinians, all Israelis, all Jews everywhere, and all Arabs everywhere on the very real beginnings of permanent peace in the Middle East.

We especially congratulate the Palestinian RCers and the Israeli RCers. They have persistently communicated with each other, encouraged each other, offered correct policy in the wide world, and fought their own and others' discouragement and despair. They have done this in the face of fierce resistance from the oppressive forces of the world. They have stood up against their own internalized patterns of oppression to do so.

Satisfaction, congratulations, and mutual appreciations are justified at this point.

The battle remains to be won, however. We now have the opportunity to furnish initiatives and clear thinking which will encourage the peace forces in the Mideast and in the world to organize effectively.

Appeared in **Present Time** No. 93, October 1993.

Public meetings need to be organized everywhere to give voice to the common people's commitment to and determination for peace. It is especially opportune for such meetings to immediately be held in Palestine and Israel, but they are needed throughout the Western and the Arab worlds.

The planning for such meetings should emphasize that these meetings are not for argument or debate in the usual sense, but only to give people an opportunity to be listened to thoroughly. It should be widely announced that no one will speak twice at such a meeting before everyone present has spoken once. Such meetings can release enormous initiative toward the solving of problems and the careful building of a peace structure. As they are carried out, they will undoubtedly serve as models for solving other difficult problems in the world.

It is important that people hopeful for peace or committed to peace have a chance to speak publicly to each other. To hear each other will firm up their resolves. It will put them in organized contact with each other. It will allow their opinions and determinations to reach the "policy-makers" of the imperialist countries.

Even people who are still fearful of peace (possibly speaking out *against* peace because of their fears) need to be listened to with respect. Only this will give them the opportunity to think their way out of the fearful dilemmas and patterned commitments of the past. Remember, few people can be "*talked* into" changing policies, but all humans can be "*listened* into" improving their policies as they think their way out of the mistakes of the past.

The forces of imperialism and their "policymakers" will still be compulsively trying to reverse the peace process in any way possible. The ruthless exploitation of workers under repressive rule is still a source of super-profits. Arms sales are still the most lucrative source for "big, quick money" for "managers" and "owners" compulsively dedicated to propping up this collapsing society in any desperate way they can.

A great network of public meetings where people are listened to with respect (no matter what they have to say), will begin to defuse the past and open the future to peace.

RCers have the skills and the knowledge to begin such initiatives. They can support and guide the organizers of such meetings. The Regional Reference Person of Israel has appealed for all RCers to do this. This appeal should be taken seriously and carried out forthwith.

The peoples of the Middle East have everything to gain from a free Palestine and a free Israel mutually supporting each other. To live in safety in Israel will free the spirits of all Israelis and all Jews everywhere in the world. The establishment of a free Palestine, soon and inevitably to be independent, will lift the spirits of all Palestinians in their exiles in the many countries of the world where they have awaited justice for so long.

Eventual repatriation to a free Palestine of all Palestinians who wish to return will give the peoples of the world and the Western governments a chance to match the support which they have previously extended to the Israelis. This support to the Israelis was based on guilt, which then was a token redress for the betrayal and oppression of the Jews by anti-Semitism in Europe and the world.

A free Palestine and a free Israel, mutually supporting each other, can quickly make the entire Holy Land a flourishing center of well-being and culture.

Apologies must be made to the Palestinians. They have been robbed of their lands, and their country has been occupied in the traditional way that imperialism has always operated. It is true that the Jewish occupation of Palestine and the founding of Israel was no worse than the robbing of the Native people of the American continents of their lands and homes and resources by the European invaders, BUT IT WAS JUST AS BAD.

The slandering of the Palestinians (and other Arabs) with a kind of ridiculous racism is no worse than the racism turned on American Natives by the European invaders of the American continents, BUT IT IS JUST AS BAD. The reality that the Jews were desperate for a homeland after the betrayals they had suffered from anti-Semitism in Europe makes the "imperialist" establishment of Israel understandable BUT NOT JUST.

The founding, establishment, and perpetuation of Israel is now a fact, comparable to the occupation of the North American continent by European-heritage people. This means that Israel cannot be destroyed. The *existence* of Israel must now be supported by all thinking humans.

The wrongs done to the Palestinians, however, must be publicly admitted, apologized for, and what restitution is possible must be made by the entire world, in particular, by the Western nations. "The unadmitted wrong can never be forgotten."

The shameful exploitation of Palestinian workers from the Occupied Territories by Israeli owning-class employers is indefensible. This state of affairs must be publicized, ended, apologized for, and guaranteed against in the future.

Working-class Israelis and working-class Palestinians have a common enemy in the oppressive class society, not only of Israel but also of the future Palestine and of the other Arab countries.

The opportunity is opening for the Palestinian working class and the Israeli working class to jointly lead a great liberation movement in all the countries of the Middle East. Such a movement will generate a great surge of progress everywhere around the world.

The signing of the Peace Accord is only a beginning, but it *is* a beginning. We call on all people of goodwill everywhere to take this breakthrough and use it to accelerate the end of all oppression world wide.

Practical Problems
on Today's Agendas

Being an Ally

For any group to progress in its liberation from oppression it is necessary that it (1) formulate a correct, workable program of liberation, (2) unite its members around that program, and (3) win allies for the group's liberation among individuals and organizations who are outside the group itself.

Acquiring allies is usually the last and the least understood part of a liberation struggle. RC discussions of liberation theory in the past have often tried to emphasize this *winning* of allies. At other times we have stressed the *exchange* of mutual support between *two or more* liberation groups who agree to support *each other's* programs.

These are not the only viewpoints from which alliances can arise. As the notion of "one for all and all for one" continues to slowly permeate our attitudes, we have tended to put forward certain *initiatives to be taken by ourselves* as allies to other groups. Such initiatives represent an important break with the "what's in it for me?" posture toward which the oppressive society has influenced us. To organize those of us *who are outside a particular group* to take initiative and become supportive allies *for members of that group* can be very effective. It is a sharp contradiction to the general selfishness and isolation which has been modelled for us and imposed upon us in the past by the oppressive societies.

Appeared in **Present Time** No. 91, April 1993.

I propose we all try to think about and plan to become role models of "effective allies for others." I propose that we not only model this but that we encourage other people to join us in playing this role as a practical route toward becoming "one for all and all for one." I propose that we plan to recruit others and expand the numbers of people doing this until, at some time in the future, there will be no human being of any age or any other characteristic that does not have other humans of different characteristics close at hand, ready to take initiative towards supporting her or him in her or his survival and goals.

To do this, we will need to think about our "constituencies" (the people to whom we shall become allies) in some organized way.

Who are the people for whom I shall begin to organize myself to be an ally?

Myself: I propose that I (and I encourage you, too, to do this for yourself) remind myself of my own innate, elegant goodness, brilliance, courage, freedom, and power. I deserve *my own* full support. In my battle against the patterns which will persistently (until they have all been discharged) tend to distort my view of myself, tend to mask and suppress my confidence, my freedom of initiative, and my power, I propose that I be *my own* excellent ally. I can do this by reminding myself repetitively of my real nature (particularly in the areas which are still tending to be most deeply invalidated by patterns). I can remind myself of my excellence, my competence, and my power. I can remind myself that reality is always supporting the upward-trend forces in my life, in spite of the incessant propaganda from the oppressive society and in spite of the dead, static persistence of my patterns. I *will* be a dependable ally to myself under all conditions.

All young people of all ages: For the world's population as a whole to eventually act rationally toward each other and toward our lovely planet, we must find a way to halt the cascade of mistreatment and false information which is flooded upon young people in their early years by the society and by the patterns of the adult population. For an adult to share an *accurate* picture of reality with a young person and explain the source of the patterned unreality which dominates the appearances of people and society, may enable the young person to hold out against the pseudo-reality of the patterned world. Reassurance (and counseling) can make a huge difference for members of this group.

All women: The female majority of the world's population has been systematically treated with unfairness, lack of respect, abuse, and exploitation at every stage of their lives. Women as well as men, *but men in particular*, can interrupt this mistreatment with a firm stand against the oppression and with firm reminders to women of their excellence. Women can be reminded of their full status as the most complex entities produced by the universe and their key roles in carrying this magnificent complexity forward into the future. Women must be allies of women. Young people must be allies of women. Men, in particular, must be allies of women. Since men in the past have been systematically trained and conditioned by the society to play the roles of oppressors to women, they are in an excellent position to be very effective in interrupting and ending the exploitation and mistreatment and in contradicting and assisting in the discharge of the women's patterns that have resulted from it.

Men: Male humans are fully qualified humans, human in every respect. They are equally intelligent with women. They have given enormous effort over the span of human existence to mastering the environments surrounding humans to produce safety, survival, and nurturance for all people. The mistakes that men have made, and sometimes persisted in, have been caused by the irrational societies and the patterns perpetuated by them. These mistakes are not the results of men's real male natures. Men are inherently brave, honest, intelligent, and responsible. Men have almost always been treated with isolation and invalidation. If men are reached for and supported by allies (other men as well as women and young people) it will make an enormous difference in men's lives. It will free them to be more effective allies for all other people.

Parents: Parents are deeply oppressed by the society *as parents.* The most important single job in the entire society is the production of new humans. This is true rationally, as human beings are far and away the most complex, valuable, and significant entities connected with the general phenomenon of life and the activities taking place around us. Even from the irrational viewpoint of the oppressive society, new humans are the source of new value, of wealth, of opportunities for profit. Any multi-national corporation would spend a hundred billion dollars to produce anything as complex and able as a human being if there were no easier way to produce one. Yet this critical work of bearing and parenting children is completely unpaid and accompanied by fatigue and desperation.

Parents are also a principal avenue for the transmission of distress to the next generation, and their efforts to avoid this and resist this role are frustrated by the oppression. Every parent deserves, and will receive in a rational society of the future, unswerving, supportive assistance from non-parents (which will be greatly to the advantage of the non-parents themselves). It will be of great assistance to the children who will tend to receive attention and companionship in the quantities they need. ("Every individual child needs at least five full-time parents.") Such real support and alliance accompanied by the organization of parent support groups and classes, parents' workshops and leadership will make the life of parents much more the joy that they have glimpsed occasionally. It will enable them to break the chain of restimulation and contagion that has passed on the patterns of the previous generations so devastatingly to date.

"Minorities in the population": Any group of people who have any physical characteristic distinguishable from the corresponding characteristic of the people around them (size, skin color, posture, facial expression, disability), has been targeted for oppression and exploitation *on the basis of that difference* by all class societies up to the present. Viewed rationally, any such differences are part of the individual uniqueness of all humans and are a source of richness and enjoyment for all people in the society. All such "minorities" have a stake in being allies *for each other*. All speakers of any languages different than the majority language of a given population and all people of any skin colors that differ from the skin color of the majority population will receive great benefit from supporting each other. It is also true that the people of the majority language and the majority skin color have equally much to gain by assuming the role of ally to, and leader in ending discrimination and mistreatment of any minority. To do so opens up the lives of the majority group to a richness of culture that they would otherwise be denied. It creates an atmosphere of safety and harmony for the people of the majority and for all others as well.

People "different" because of language, religion, or culture: People with such differences may not always be a minority group. They may sometimes be a majority of the population, but when a different "official" language, culture, or religion has been designated, they are then often oppressed for failure to conform. To be an ally to people of such a group one can take an interest in the culture, language, or religion. One can inform the rest of the population about the culture or religion. One can learn the language, speak it, and treat it with respect. One can organize mutual celebration of cultural events by people of both cultures and insist that the laws and customs of the political or community organizations do not discriminate against one or another.

"People who are acting out past hurts in ways that set them apart from the rest of the population": Much of such distressed behavior is often proclaimed as "rational" or "free choice" by its victims and carriers, since its source in distress patterns is not universally understood or agreed to in the society as yet. Sexual preferences or practices are still widely debated. Paedophilia is generally understood to be dangerous to children but still has some defenders. All of these, and even such a pattern as "compulsive serial murderer," which is generally agreed to be irrational and dangerous, are best handled by alliances rather than by criticism or punishment. The kind and amount of effective counseling which is necessary to free such a person from the compulsive patterns of behavior is not likely to be understood without the knowledge of RC. Such counseling is not likely to be available with the necessary skill and resource even if knowledge of RC exists. A person with such a pattern may necessarily have to be segregated for the protection of others until the resources can be brought to bear for the complete discharge of the pattern. Yet a real solution for this dilemma requires that someone (all the rest of us) think in terms of being an ally to the person who is thus being separated by the results of hurt from the rest of humankind.

What actions can we take in the direction of being a good ally to everybody? What do you think of the following?

1. *Listen* to the person tell about what it is like for her or him to be herself or himself, to be a young person, a woman, a man. *Listen* to what it's like to be a member of a minority. *Listen* to what it's like to live with the particular distress.

2. Specifically offer oneself as an ally to the person, making as deep a commitment as one can honestly do at that point.

3. Counsel, and commit oneself to counsel, on one's thoughts and feelings about being an ally in order to become more rational and more effective in that role.

4. Promise and carry through some organization of other people as a *group* of allies who will offer support, who will take action to change the situation, who will act to reduce the isolation, who will interrupt the patterns of oppression.

(I would propose that allies not "wait" for the oppressed group to tell them what to do to be helpful. In fact, I would propose that allies not allow the oppressed group to exercise any veto on the allies' planning and action. The internalized oppression of the oppressed group may lead to too timid or too limited activity in such a case. The allies need to take initiatives simply from the correctness of the position they have reached from their own thinking, not waiting for their actions to be requested nor their thinking approved of by the oppressed group.)

5. Respond aggressively to every instance of oppression. Speak out and invite other people to join the alliance. Carry on education for our policies as "allies" among the general public.

Reclaiming our full power certainly will imply independent initiative on our parts *wherever situations need change.* We can not only "be on everyone's side," we can be self-starting activist allies on everyone's side.

Updating Jewish Liberation

The thinking of the people of the world has advanced and is advancing on many issues. The ending of the Cold War, the halt of the nuclear arms race, fierce resistance to the economic difficulties presented by the collapsing of the general society—all indicate a basic shift in the climate of world opinion.

In the past, the public attitude toward the systematically organized and repeated oppression of the Jewish people was one sensitive indicator of the general state of world opinion. (A similar "indicator" role has been played in the past by public attitudes towards the oppression of Indian and Pakistani people in East Africa and the oppression of overseas Chinese in Southwest Asia.)

There are many indications that persecution of Jews (anti-Semitism) as a tool for fragmenting people's resistance to general economic exploitation is no longer able to play the role assigned to it by the oppressive societies in the past. Recently, the reactionary forces in Eastern Europe, freed from their previous formal suppression by the Soviet regimes, attempted to create neo-Nazi movements and revive anti-Semitism throughout Germany and Eastern Europe. This attempt was opposed by mass demonstrations of very large numbers of ordinary people. Attempts at reviving the circulation of scurrilous anti-Jewish slanders in the United States (while frightening to people who had never before

Appeared in **Present Time** No. 91, April 1993.

experienced it in *their* lifetimes) has been almost completely ineffective.

The current situation is by far the most favorable for Jewish liberation that it has ever been. We have a glowing opportunity to bring Jewish liberation policies and practices up-to-date.

TAKING INITIATIVE BY GENTILE ALLIES OF JEWS

The spread of correct policies from the RC initiatives of twenty years ago has created a very substantial number of informed people in the population who recognize that anti-Jewish oppression is not basically directed against Jews but against *all* progressive people's forces. Many more Gentiles than ever before are now ready to be active against oppressiveness directed at Jews. It is time that we inform, encourage, and organize to take initiatives in this area.

The organization of "Allies of Jews" support groups, classes, and workshops can become part of the agenda of every RC Community. With a little experience and training on this RC level, these groups can be extended into the wide world. The tactic of organizing parallel workshops for Jews and one other oppressed section of the population has proven very successful. These workshops have separate leaderships for each group. They have roughly equal numbers of Jews and non-Jews. Jews and African-Americans, Jews and men, Jews and working-class people, Jews and women, Jews and Asians, Jews and middle-class people, Jews and owning-class people, Jews and Gay men and Lesbians, Jews and disabled people, etc.— all can learn a great deal about liberation from each other and can improve their alliances deeply. Most of the work with the two groups is done separately, but they meet together for part of the workshop, hear reports from the other group, and exchange leaders for at least a class session.

It should be a goal in every Community to establish at least one wide-world organization of "Gentiles against the oppression of Jews" which is ready to take action against any incidents or threats of violence. It can and should act on its own initiative, in contact with but not dependent on or limited by any of the Jewish organizations. This is especially crucial in dealing with anti-Israel attacks. The Gentile organizations must be free to be critical of any mistaken policies such as have often been forced on Israel by its dependence on the U.S. and other western imperialists for arms and financing. The Gentile organizations must at the same time insist that the world guarantee Israel's permanent existence.

GENTILES COUNSELING JEWS ON THEIR INTERNALIZED OPPRESSION

Informed allies outside an oppression are always able to be very effective in counseling people subject to a particular oppression. This is always true, and it can be dramatically effective with the internalized oppression of Jews because of the key role of isolation in this internalized oppression. Gentile Co-Counselors who have informed themselves of the particulars of Jewish oppression will be able to be especially effective because their very existence and activity is a sharp contradiction to the distress.

If Gentile counselors keep in mind that the isolation of Jews has been repeatedly reinforced by the historical experiences that lie behind the Jewish people, they can be far more effective in contradicting it. Gentile Co-Counselors who think of the Holocaust (six million Jews dead in the Nazi death camps) as only "something that happened a long time ago," will not be effective. Although most Jews presently alive did not experience the Holocaust directly, it became a rigid policy for them to be forced to listen over and over to terrifying messages about the Holocaust, to have to read the ghastly records and see movies about the inhuman things that happened. This was made a deliberate policy toward the young people by their frightened elders and leaders "lest the youth forget." This has left a layer of terror on almost every Jew in the present generations of Jews. It is ready to discharge, but it needs to be contradicted actively and realistically. (A flat personal guarantee by the Gentile counselor to take personal initiative against any anti-Semitic activity in the counselor's city can have this effect.)

Gentile counselors can understandably but mistakenly assume that Jewish clients "must surely feel good about themselves" because of their obvious success and competence at their jobs, professions, leadership, initiatives, and efforts. Gentile counselors must not remain ignorant nor forget that most of these accomplishments took place under the lash of terror and under pressure from their families and people to see it as "a necessary requirement if you are to survive."

Gentile counselors, seeing the attractive appearance of their Jewish clients, (sometimes enviously), must face and realize that there is heavy conditioning (at least among most Western Jews), to associate themselves with the insulting adjectives that have been rehearsed at them and internalized, adjectives such as "dirty," "disgusting," "greedy," etc.

Gentile counselors should keep in mind that it is probably going to be "hard" for a Jewish client to really believe that the Gentile counselor likes him or her, wants to be with him or her, and respects him or her. Correctly informed and keeping these things in mind, the Gentile counselor can be much more effective.

JEWS BATTLING THE *INTERNALIZED* OPPRESSION

Jewish RCers as a group have been outstanding in their acceptance of RC, their application of it to their own re-emergence, and their leadership in strengthening the Communities, both in numbers and activity. Many of the following proposals have been initiated or carried out in one or more Communities already. Proposals for moving against the internalized oppression need to be prefaced with recognition of the outstanding work that has already been accomplished. I make these proposals because more improvement is needed but also because these ideas have not been systematically disseminated everywhere as yet.

The heart of the effective direction for cleaning the *internalized* oppression out of our policies and practices is in the "Jewish Commitment" (against internalized oppression). This says, **"From this moment on I will greet every person I meet as if she or he were *eager* to be my warm, close, dependable friend and ally under all conditions."**

It is true, regardless of all the propaganda and conditioning, that any Jewish person is just exactly a human being, no different than any other human being in the world in any essential. Such a Jewish person is possessed of one or another of several varieties of Jewish cultures. These cultures are partly made up of valuable, estimable, greatly-to-be-cherished-and-shared-with-the-rest-of-the-world components. Also, however, they partly consist of the distress patterns and distressed roles forced upon the Jewish people in the past under various conditions of extreme oppression. Because they were laid in as distress recordings, they have been clung to as "the only way to survive" in spite of their repeated failures in the past to do anything but damage survival.

197

Is assimilation and concealment of one's Jewish identity a successful survival tactic? In certain crisis situations with completely irrational people, and very briefly, perhaps yes, but not in general, not long-range. Once all oppressions are ended there will certainly be no obligation on anyone to stay with any particular identification. We work in our sessions to give up particular identifications even at present. (In a completely safe, warmly-supportive situation, a Jewish client can get a glimpse outside the oppression and discharge voluminously by announcing, "I am not a Jew.") But concealment and denial are not effective tactics for the liberation of the group.

Part of the general pressure of classism on all the population is to keep greed as the dominant motivation for all people. Classism proposes as a survival tactic the attainment of economic success. Workers are at least to dream of climbing up into the middle class or even into the owning class. This also comes as a "policy" from Jewish "community leaders" everywhere in the Diaspora.

Supporting the powers-that-be and making oneself indispensable to rulers have been forced on the Jews in exile for over a thousand years, yet in every generation outstanding Jews have repudiated these goals. These requirements are in conflict with the basic strengths of Jewish culture—the esteeming of every person, the insistence on justice for *all* people. It is not required nor is it good survival for Jews to put "climbing up" economically at the heart of their survival program. It is no longer necessary nor will it work for Jews to support the conservative economic forces in their countries.

I propose that Jews both within RC and in the wide world organize Jewish support groups which publicize their existence by taking correct attitudes on *all* liberation issues. I propose they contact the other groups that suffer oppression in the present societies—the young people, the working class, the people of color, etc.—and explain their program for liberation for Jews. I propose that they offer support in helping the other group to organize for the liberation of *their* group. I suggest they propose an alliance between the Jews and each of the other groups on all the issues on which they are in agreement. I propose that Jews play this role inside the RC Community, take the initiative toward all other groups, and help the other groups organize their programs, meetings, workshops, support groups, and classes. In all this I propose that the activity of the Jews be public and that they serve as a model of organization, not as "people behind the scenes."

I propose that Jewish liberation, both within RC and in the wide world, become in every way a model of a liberation movement, showing each of the other movements the possibility for rational and far-reaching success. I propose that Jewish liberation workers initiate contact with all other liberation forces, encourage them, assist them, and organize coalitions with them.

I propose that Gentile RCers become experts on Jewish history, Jewish oppression, Jewish liberation, and Jewish struggle. I propose that we Gentile Co-Counselors become expert at helping Jews discharge all phases of their internalized oppression while they advance to proud, relaxed, flourishing, uninhibited confidence.

Toward More Rational Policies on Eliminating Distress Around Incest

We can be proud of the leadership which RCers have taken in initiating the discharge of distress caused by early sexual abuse. This general initiative quickly led to tackling the distress around *incest*, the sexual abuse perpetrated within one's family. The effect of discharging and re-evaluating on incest has almost always brought substantial benefits in terms of the client becoming at ease with himself or herself, recovering a dependable picture of his or her own inherent goodness, and in restoring broken relationships.

It quickly became apparent that "perpetrators" of abuse had always first been "victims," that the patterns of hurting others had always first been laid in by the individual perpetrator having been abused himself or herself. Then later, he or she would fall into "acting out" the other end of the pattern.

As support groups, classes, and workshops on early sexual abuse in general, and on incest in particular, multiplied, it was evident that these distresses were much more common in our cultures than had been suspected. It was also discovered that abuse had often taken bizarre forms. "Ritual" abuse was reported, involving religious-like ceremonies. "Memories" were reported of being forced as children to make pornographic movies.

Appeared in **Present Time** No. 92, July 1993.

[At one point, an unexpected source of strange "memories" was revealed. This consists of an infant being *told* by a patterned adult that the infant had participated in vicious abuse of others—very often the account involved the death of another child with the listening child being blamed. Being told this with great intensity by the pattern of the terrified adult leaves the infant with a recording which she or he usually internalizes *as having actually participated in the events of the abuser's tale.* These patterns tend to remain occluded until the victim, now grown to adulthood, finds himself or herself *alone with an infant.* Then the recording is triggered and the one-time victim now becomes the "perpetrator" of this kind of abuse on the new infant. He or she tells the infant, with terrifying tension, the story of how *this* infant participated in the abuse, and often the death, of another child. It seems that a whole network has thus arisen, spreading widely across a whole country, or perhaps the world, where no such events actually occurred (at least for many generations), but where terror and compulsive "belief" leave harmful myths and distress on growing numbers of people, since each perpetrator can "infect" several others.]

The discharge and re-evaluation that has been achieved in the sessions, support groups, and workshops on incest has been of great benefit to the people who have participated. A movement in the wide world to expose the sexual abuse and incest phenomenon arose not much later than the one that began in RC and was quickly expanded. Publicity about such mistreatment of children led to improvement in the treatment of children by social workers. It gained children new credibility in court cases and resulted in many other good developments.

So far, so good.

ALERTNESS AGAINST PATTERNS

Patterns and patterned motivations tend to be present around any re-emergence activity because of the very nature of what we are re-emerging from. Certain distortions and patterned motivations tend to lurk around and affect these activities, certainly in the wide world, and to some extent in RC. The basic goal of discharge and re-evaluation—that is, to become free of distress and rational in one's thinking—occasionally becomes supplanted or modified by an attachment to "being a victim." A support group, furnishing the "safety" of being with other people with similar past distresses, allows one to feel safe and discharge. It also can be misused to reinforce an identity of being a "victim," with the patterned "rewards" of feeling sorry for oneself, of claiming sympathy from others, or of being furnished a dependable "excuse" for not taking charge of and for not being responsible for progress in one's life.

It has been the experience of those of us who have led workshops on sexual abuse, including incest, that clients in demonstrations which we have done are often eager to shower us with gratitude and attach a "dependency" to us. Not often, but sometimes, the results of good discharge at a workshop have resulted in a rigid "grateful" dependency on the workshop leader rather than in building strong support groups and Wygelian leaders' groups in the Co-Counselor's local Community.

RC has a basic "folk wisdom" about patterned identifications, including identifications of oneself as a "victim." This wisdom can be summarized as, "Claim it temporarily. Discharge it thoroughly. Throw it away." In some cases the relief at openly presenting and discharging on the distress of sexual abuse has become subverted to clinging to the identification of "victim" for the client and of "guru-hood" for the "expert" leader.

THE CORRECT USE OF FANTASY

The use of fantasy has been developed in RC as a powerful, useful tool to begin to lift occluded memories out of occlusion, to give more flexibility in the creation of the contradictions to the distress that will make discharge possible, and to circumvent patterned strictures on the client, which may have been installed with the distress itself. Fantasy has *never* been proposed in RC as a means of establishing *what actually happened* in the occluded past. It is totally unreliable for this purpose.

The reason for this unreliability is the *suggestibility* of the human mind, particularly when under stress or subject to irrational motivations. Much of the pseudo-reality, which surrounds us like a great fog in our cultures, consists of false information that *we were told was true* by someone we trusted. We were then motivated to continue to believe by threats of punishment or rejection if we did not.

(A great part of our work in developing a useful theory and workable practice in RC has been to distinguish between this "pseudo-reality," which has been pushed upon us by these past pressures, and the actual reality of what is going on and has really been going on in the past.)

When a client or Co-Counselor "remembers" an incident of being abused, what is the correct role for the counselor? It is certainly *not* to deny the validity of the person's "memory." That the client has been able to bring up the story indicates that it is important to his or her progress. To invalidate the story as offered is, in effect, to invalidate the client, to make the process the client is engaged in more difficult, and to restimulate any rejection and unaware responses which the client has experienced in the past.

It is the job of the counselor to be interested in and accepting of the client's account as a useful version of what the client is trying to remember and discharge. It is *not* the job of the counselor to declare the memory "authentic." The counselor does not have, and probably never will have, any way of knowing whether that particular version of the client's narrative is "authentic" or not.

The job of the Co-Counseling pair is to work together to contradict the distress and secure discharge. The continuing part of their job is to secure more discharge and secure more discharge and secure more discharge. Their job eventually becomes to "clean up the incident."

If the client begs for reassurance from the counselor with such phrases as, "It really did happen?" or, "Don't you believe me?" or, "This can't be true, can it?" the counselor can simply say, "Let's assume it's true, for now, and see how much discharge we can get," and then proceed to find, create, and offer contradictions to the distress that will bring voluminous discharge.

Fantasizing is a powerful and useful tool because of its flexibility. It is *not* a tool for determining the "validity," or settling on any "final" version of what actually happened in the past.

As this great "underground" mass of sexual mistreatment distress of infants, children, youth, and adults has been revealed and explored in the wide world, certain patterned developments have come into prominence. The theories that guide most psychologists and psychiatrists, which they have acquired in their "professional training," are often bizarre, to say the least. Besides the basic role of all aspects of the "mental health" system of justifying and enforcing oppression, the theories taught these "professionals" are unscientific in the extreme.

One of the most popular of these unexamined, unconfirmed theories is often called the theory of "repression." No experimental validation of this theory has ever been done, but it has been passed hand to hand by psychologists and educational institutions as if it were confirmed reality. This theory can be and often is used to "validate" the wildest fantasies of individuals (which are really offered by the fantasizing person in an attempt to get some distress out of occlusion in order that it can be contradicted and discharged). When these fantasies are thus "confirmed" (instead of the distress in them being contradicted and discharged), the fantasizing person becomes "stuck" with the "confirmed" fantasies. In this "stuck" condition, such people, often in good faith, repeat these fantasies as realities. They even write books about them, and other distressed people who read the books and are "suggestible" are encouraged to evolve and proclaim similar fantasies.

Law enforcement personnel to whom these fantasies are offered can be motivated to accept them as "confirmed." To accept and proclaim them can bring publicity to the law-enforcement-person from sensation-seeking reporters and can lend pseudo-importance to the law enforcement person's otherwise often hum-drum and unappreciated work.

"Psychologists" can then often be gotten to confirm the "probable reality" of these fantasies, using such unverified theories as the one about "repression." This can give the psychologists an aura of "expertise" and create work and fees for them that otherwise would not be available.

Certain TV talk shows can then bring people caught in such dramatizing distresses onto their shows, where they can be encouraged to attack individuals in their lives or in the news with accusations which the TV shows hope will titillate their audiences and expand their ratings.

CREATING A NEW CHANNEL FOR CONDITIONING PEOPLE TO DISTRUST EACH OTHER

For three-quarters of a century whole national populations have been "handled" by installing and manipulating a conditioned terror of and hatred of "Communism." Huge profits have been amassed by arms manufacturers, and national elections have been won by sleazy candidates by appealing to people's fears of the "Communist enemy." It is finally becoming clear to large numbers of people that the policies of "anti-Communism" and the policies of the "Cold War" were fraudulent. With hindsight it is plain that these policies were created to plunder the nations' own populations and distract people from taking charge of their own affairs. "Anti-Communism" was used again and again to prevent people from using good judgment about their own national interests.

A number of intelligent people have speculated that publicity about the mistreatment of children (including the sexual abuse of children) is being used in an attempt to create a new source of suspicion in the popular mind. People are being encouraged to suspect their neighbors' "evil hidden natures," somewhat in the way people were earlier encouraged to suspect their neighbors of being "witches." This way of keeping people afraid of each other and therefore discouraged and afraid about working cooperatively together in their own interests can be seized upon and promoted. This can be done by law enforcement agencies, mistrained and misguided psychologists, people of certain "fundamentalist" religious beliefs, and certain ordinary people who happen to be ridden by chronic patterns of resentment which are seeking a safe object upon which to focus their hatred and terror.

I do not think that RCers can tolerate falling into these errors in any degree.

I think it is crucial that RC take a firm stand against using fantasies as evidence for what is or has been reality.

I think we need to remind ourselves and other people that reaching negative judgments by any group against any other group, or against individuals, can only be a patterned activity. Our business is not to spread distress but to discharge and eliminate it.

An investigative reporter, Lawrence Wright, has written a two-part article in the *New Yorker* of May 17th and May 24th, 1993. The article describes in detail what happened to a very "respectable," conservative family in Olympia, Washington, USA, when fantasies were accepted uncritically in the name of the theory of "repression." Some mentalities of law enforcement personnel and of "fundamentalist" Christian believers were allowed to operate in the investigation as official policies. I heartily recommend that you read these articles. You will find them available in public libraries if you do not have these *New Yorkers* in your possession. The articles are called: "Remembering Satan—Part 1" and "Remembering Satan—Part 2."

To the extent that any slightest trace of this patterned clutter happening in the wide world has become attached to any of our activities in RC, we need to clean things up. Our policies must remain dedicated to reality, to establishing and proclaiming the basic goodness of human beings, and to the workability and effectiveness of the re-emergence process.

A Commitment for Persons of German-Speaking Heritage

German-speaking people are in a peculiar, specific, and different situation in regard to their re-emergence than people of most other cultures in the world today.

It was common in the past—in the slave societies, in feudal societies, and in early capitalist-imperialist societies—for whole peoples to be committed, due to their social conditioning, to the anti-human programs of the ruling classes.

Peoples of all cultures in the early twentieth century were pressured by the most backward elements of their ruling classes to be committed as a whole to the most oppressive programs, including class oppression, racism, sexism, anti-Semitism, oppression of the disabled, and oppression of the young and of the old. Extreme forms of these oppressions, including genocide, destruction of indigenous cultures, occupation of homelands, massive relocations, and executions of resisters without trial, have been part of the historical background of most peoples.

It is crucial for the full re-emergence of every group to acquaint itself with *all* aspects of its history and to discharge thoroughly on them. (From our experience with present-time techniques and the Reality Agreement, this counseling often

Appeared in **Present Time** No. 97, October 1994. (Translation of the following article.)

goes better putting direct attention on the wonderful things about that people's history and culture while at the same time avoiding any pretense about *anything* that has happened in the past.)

All peoples of the twentieth century fought against these oppressive tendencies and resisted them to a greater or lesser degree. In only a few countries did the mass of people succumb to these pressures and participate in them as a group. The Japanese people and the Italian people, for example, have much to answer for in their toleration of the invasions of China and of Ethiopia.

It is also true, and too little noted, that large numbers of German-speaking people fought against the policies of Hitler—fought to defend the lives of the victims of Nazism and often lost their own lives in the defense of justice and freedom.

The great majority of the German-speaking peoples of the world, however, supported the policies of Nazism in their most inhuman forms. This was a glaring anachronism for an educated, industrially-developed people in the middle of the twentieth century. They separated themselves from these policies—not with bravery and honor—but only with the opportunism made possible by the Nazi defeat. The policy makers for the ruling classes of the United States, Great Britain, and France supported this opportunism and did not require the profound re-evaluation needed for the German people to reclaim their honor. In the Soviet-sponsored regime of East Germany, the public pronouncements against the Nazi heritage were much clearer, but the actual re-education and re-evaluation achieved has been revealed to be inadequate by the events in East Germany following the unification.

In this century, the re-evaluation by the German-speaking peoples of their relationship to the Nazi program is an unfinished, urgently needed process.

The importance of this for those who were alive during the Nazi rule may be immediately clear to most of us. The importance for subsequent generations of discharging completely in this area may not be quite so evident. It is, however, just as important.

Although the younger generations may have had no direct hand in collaborating with the Nazis, they have grown up in a society with pervasive "denial" and pretense in regard to this history. As young people, they sensed that something was very wrong—they could see that in the adults around them—but were denied access to information (and attention) that would have made it possible to discharge on what actually happened (something we know that *every* human longs to do). Furthermore, they are now seeing increasingly clearly the ongoing effects of the Nazi belief in the present period.

No commitment to an individual German-speaking person's pride, including a claim to his or her full humanness, can avoid a pledge to actively undo the continuing pro-oppressive elements of the German culture.

Draft Commitment for Peoples of German-Speaking Heritage

I am a German-speaking human.

I am inherently fully human in every way.

I denounce every wrong that was done or participated in by German-speaking peoples during the Nazi period as I denounce all other instances of oppression in the world.

I will wage unceasing battle to eliminate every trace of the pernicious effects of Nazism in German-speaking societies and cultures and in our relations with each other and with all other peoples of the world.

As I carry out this activity, I will be proud. I will be an ally to all peoples of the world. I will be a dependable force to eliminate all oppressions and will thus deserve everyone's love, support, and, in particular, my own complete pride in myself.

Ein Versprechen für Menschen deutschsprachiger Herkunft

Deutschsprachiege Menschen befinden sich heute in Bezug auf ihr Wiederauftauchen in einer ganz bestimmten und gleichzeitig anderen Situation als Menschen der meisten anderen Kulturen der Welt.

In der Vergangenheit—in Sklavengesellschaften, in Feudalsystemen und in früheren kapitalistisch-imperialistischen Systemen—haben sich ganze Völker üblicherweise unmenschlichen Programmen verschrieben und zwar auf Grund ihrer gesellschaftlichen Erziehung und der Programme der herrschenden Klasse.

Im 20. Jahrhundert wurden Menschen aller Kulturen von den rückständigsten Elementen ihrer herrschenden Klasse dazu gedrängt, als ganze Völker äußerst ybterdrückende Programme zu unterstützen und zwar Klassenunterdrückung, Rassismus, Sexismus, Antisemitismus, Unterdrückung von Behinderten, Unterdrückung von jungen und von alten Menschen, u.a. Extreme Formen dieser Unterdrückung—Völkermord, Vernichtung von einheimischen Kulturen, Besetzung von Heimatländern, Maßenübersiedlungen, und Hinrichtungen von Menschen im Widerstand ohne Gerichtsverfahren—waren Teil der historischen Vergangenheit der meisten Völker.

Appeared in **Present Time** No. 97, October 1994.

Es ist kritisch für das volle Wiederauftauchen einer jeden Gruppe sich mit *allen* Aspekten ihrer Geschichte auseinander-zusetzen und darüber gründlich zu entlasten. (Wir wissen schon folgendes von unserer Erfahrung mit den Counsel-methoden "Aufmerksamkeit auf die Gegenwart richten" und "Wirklichkeits-Abkommen": Das Counseln geht besser, wenn man den wunderbaren Seiten der Geschichte und Kultur der Menschen direkte Aufmerksamkeit schenkt und gleichzeitig *nichts* von dem verleugnet, das in der Vergangenheit passiert ist.)

All Völker des 20. Jahrhunderts kämften gegen diese unterdrückenden Tendenzen an und leisteten—zu einem größeren oder geringeren Ausmaß—Widerstand dagegen. Nur in wenigen Ländern hat sich der überwiegender Teil der Menschen diesem Druck unterworfen und als ganze Gruppe daran teilgenommen. Das japanische Volk und das italienische Volk z. B. sind noch eine Antwort darauf schuldig, daß sie die Invasion von China und von Ethiopien zugelassen haben.

Es ist auch wahr und zu wenig anerkannt, daß eine große Zahl deutschsprachieger Menschen gegen die Politik Hitlers ankämpften—um das Leben von den Opfern des NS-Re-gimes zu retten—und dadurch ihr eigenes Leben bei ihrem Kampf für Freiheit und Gerechtigkeit verloren.

Die große Mehrheit der deutschsprachigen Bevölkerung der Welt jedoch, unterstützte die Politik des Nazi Regimes in ihrer äußerst unmenschlichen Form. Sie distanzierte sich von dieser Politik nicht mit Tapferkeit und Ehre, sondern erst—opportunistisch—durch die Zerschlagung des Nazi Regimes. Die Regierungstreibenden der herrschenden Klassen der Vereinigten Staaten, Groß Britaniens und Frankreichs unterstützten diesen Opportunismus und verlangten keine grundsätzliche Neubewertung der NS-Zeit, die notwendig für das deutsche Volk gewesen wäre, seine Ehre für sich zurückzugewinnen. Im von der Soviet Union unterstützen Regime der DDR waren die öffentlichen Aussagen und Erklärungen gegen das Erbe der NS-Zeit viel deutlicher, aber der tatsächlich erreichte Einstellungswandel hat sich als unzureichend erwiesen, wie die Erreignisse in Ostdeutschland seit der Wiedervereinigung Deutschlands zeigen.

In diesem Jahrhundert steht ein unfertiger, dringend notwendiger Prozeß für die deutschsprachigen Menschen an, nämlich die Neuauswertung ihrer Beziehung zur NS-Politik.

Die Wichtigkeit dieser Neuawswertung für diejenigen, die während der Nazi-Herrschaft am Leben waren, ist wahrscheinlich für die meisten von uns klar verständlich. Die Wichtigkeit für nachfolgende Generationen, auf diesem Gebiet vollständig zu entlasten, mag nicht ganz so offensichtlich sein. Es ist dies jedoch genau so wichtig.

Obwohl die jüngere Generation nicht direkt an der Kollaboration mit den Nazis deteiligt war, ist sie in einer Gesellschaft aufgewachsen, in welcher der Geschichte der NS-Vergangenheit nicht offen in die Augen geschaut wird. Als junge Menschen haben sie gespürt, daß etwas sehr falsch war—sie haben es in den Erwachsenen, die um sie herum waren, gesehen. Es wurden ihnen jedoch die Informationen und die Auferksamkeit vorenthalten, die notwendig gewesen wären, darüber zu entlasten was tatsächlich passierte (wir wissen, daß sich jeder Mensch danach sehnt, das zu entlasten). Darüberhinaus beobachten sie jetzt zunehmend deutlich die immer noch vorhandenen Auswirkungen des national-sozialistischen Gedankengutes in der Gegenwart.

Kein Versprechen, das vom Stolz und vom Wiedererlangen der vollkommenen Menschlichkeit eines deutschsprachigen

Menschen handelt, kann ohne ein bestimmtes Gelöbnis auskommen. Nämlich das Gelöbnis, der in der deutschsprachiegn Kultur immer noch bestehenden Tendenz, Unterdrückung zu betreiben, aktiv ein Ende zu bereiten.

Entwirf eines Versprechens
für Menschen deutschsprachiger Herkunft

Ich bin ein/e deutschsprachiege/r Frau/Mann.

Ich bin durch und durch menschlich in jeder Hinsicht.

Ich verurteile öffentlich jedes Unrecht, das in der Nazi-Zeit von deutschsprachigen Menschen verübt wurde oder an welchem diese beteiligt waren, und ich verurteile auch alle anderen Fällen von Unterdrückung in der Welt.

Ich werde einen unaufhörlichen Kampf führen, um jede Spur der verderblichen Auswirkungen des Nationalsozialismus zu beseitigen und das ist in der deutschsprachigen Gesellschaft und Kultur, in unseren Beziehungen zueinander und in unseren Beziehungen zu allen anderen Menschen der Erde.

Während ich das tue werde ich stolz sein. Ich werde allen Menschen der Welt ein/e Verbündete/r sein. Ich werde eine verläßliche Kraft sein, jegliche Unterdrückung zu beenden und somit die Liebe aller Menschen, deren Hilfe und deren— und besonders auch meinen eigenen—ganzen Stolz auf mich verdienen.

Understanding
Our Progress
As We Make It

How Complex and Abstract Should I Make My Art?

Dear Harvey,

I have resisted writing you because I know you are very busy. But I am doing so because I was unable to ask you a question (that has been on my mind for a long while) at Prindle Pond. So here goes: Should artists who create "modern art" (abstract paintings, or, in my case, music that is non-tonal) be concerned if their work is so complex that it simply restimulates their audience? In other words, what good is art, what useful function does it serve if it only makes someone feel stupid, uninformed, and unconnected to the artist? Should an artist consider what we in RC know about the learning process—that new information can only be understood in context and relationship to what one already knows, and that the learner must be relaxed, feel safe, and receive love from the source of information? To what extent should this affect the content of an artist's work? Finally, what functions does complex artwork serve in a collapsing society where many people are (or will be) concerned mainly with survival issues (food, shelter, etc.) and don't have much attention for much else?

I will continue to think about this, but I would like to hear your thoughts on this, I think, important matter. Any response will be deeply appreciated.

Whit Brown
Somerville, Massachusetts, USA

Appeared in **Present Time** No. 95, April 1994.

Dear Whit,

I also find your questions thoughtful and thought-provoking. I assume you've read my article "The Good and the Great in Art," so you know the distinction I attempt to make between non-art (which expresses nothing new but only what has gone before and is therefore not creative), poor art (which deals creatively, at least to some extent, with its subject but presents the distress in the culture or of the artist as if it were reality), good art (which is creative and may deal both with distress and new creativity but makes the distinction between actual reality and the distressed versions of it), and great art (which presents newly created concepts).

Your question about the value of abstract or very complex art that is too complex to be appreciated by most people is a different question. Here, I think, one must allow for the many different levels of audience that any artistic endeavor will impact. I think the overall tendency on the part of art will always be toward more complexity, which includes the possibility of more and more abstraction. I tend to become quite bored with the drumming of many Native cultures on this continent and when I am invited to participate in the drumming must resist very hard my impulses to introduce some more complex beats to "fancy it up a little." Similarly, most rock and roll music seems to me boring and resonating with patterns. And I'm certain many very skillful musicians would feel that my desire to have something of Mozart playing in the background almost all the time is too dull for their tastes.

I think a good artist will create with many different audiences in mind at different times, and only the more limited artists will stick to one narrow channel as they strive to be creative. Picasso ceaselessly experimented with pushing the frontiers of visual art outward, but occasionally painted something so elegant and simple that everyone who saw it was moved.

I think to work on the frontiers of art in a time of a collapsing society and great hardship for the people still makes sense. Good work done in this period will be remembered and appreciated when there is more leisure and security. But I think if I were an artist I would broaden my palette and also do some things that are easy to be widely understood, and hopefully have a message of confidence, cheer, and bravery for the people in the middle of struggle.

It's all right to create for other artists as well as for your next door neighbor; it will tend to motivate you in an upward trend direction. But you need not be disappointed if your appreciative audience is smaller in the one case than the other.

Harvey

What Do We Mean
By "Class"?

Dear Harvey,

I am writing to continue our discussion about "class."

As part of a joint venture between the IRS and the union I work for, I co-taught a course in "conflict management" in February to a group of file clerks and their supervisors at the IRS Kansas City Service Center. In one part of the course, I asked each of them to talk about the characteristics they identified as important in their background, including religion, part of the country, race, ethnic background, and class (so that we could discuss whether discordant non-verbal messages linked to these characteristics might be messing up their communications). From the information I had about the group, my guess was that they were solidly in the working class. But none of them could relate to this term: a couple identified themselves as "lower class" and the rest did not come up with any identity. My suspicion is that this uneasiness with the concept of class is very widespread in the U.S. today.

*After I received your letter, I glanced through some of my books related to social and economic theory, including some Marxist writers, to see what they had to say about class. (I have not kept up-to-date on the latest developments in the field I studied over fifteen years ago in graduate school, but I have kept my favorite books.) I found **Contested Terrain**, a book by Richard Edwards, one of my*

Appeared in **Present Time** No. 96, July 1994.

professors and a man whose thinking and writings influenced me a lot. I had another surprise when I re-read Chapter 10 of his book and realized that many of my present general ideas about class fit precisely within the framework that Edwards lays out. I guess his ideas made sense to me at the time I first read them and my experience since then has borne him out. I am sending you the book because if you aren't familiar with it you may be interested in seeing how he applies historical analysis to twentieth century capitalist development in the U.S.

Edwards grapples with the problem of naming classes on page 185 and comes up with the descriptive but unpleasant term "fraction." I do not think RC needs any complicated definitions of class, but I do think we need clear and consistent definitions. In my experience, seeing the "middle class" as a sub-set of the "working class" is not a commonly agreed-upon concept, and moreover it may feel counter-intuitive and confusing for people. I tend to feel I am a middle-class trade union activist who represents many middle-class trade union members. The RC Union Activists' Commitment can only be my own if middle-class unionists are included in the working class, but I am not sure that a lot of RCers interpret it that way. It goes against widespread understanding of the word class, as vague as this understanding is, to define one class, the middle class, as being within another class, the working class, but to give both groupings the same title of "class." I think most people who have a concept that they are in the middle class believe that they are therefore not in the working class, and vice-versa.

RC theory and the RC Community are tremendously important to me. The whole tone of my life has been different since my first RC class eight years ago. I attribute the good discharge I've done and information I've received and formulated from RC as the reason that I got my current job, that I've done it so well, and that I've continually developed my organizing skills. It is a wonderful thing you have done in building a world community and helping others acquire/unearth the tools and understanding to do the same.

Here are several of my favorite economic and union history books for inclusion on the list that you suggested might be circulated among trade union leaders. (I would like to receive the list even though I do not consider myself a "younger" union leader. And I must let you know that I was surprised by the assumptions I read into your letter that I must be young, inexperienced, and ignorant of theory. If I am right about these assumptions, I wonder why?)

Richard Edwards, <u>Contested Terrain: The Transformation of the Workplace in the Twentieth Century</u>, Basic Books, Inc., 1979.

Peter Friedlander, <u>The Emergence of a UAW Local, 1936-1939: A Study in Class and Culture</u>, University of Pittsburgh Press, 1975.

Richard Drinnon, <u>Rebel in Paradise: A Biography of Emma Goldman</u>, Harper & Row, Publishers, 1976.

David Brody, <u>Steelworkers in America: The Nonunion Era</u>, Harper & Row, Publishers, 1969.

Barbara Kingsolver, <u>Holding the Line: Women in the Great Arizona Mine Strike of 1983</u>, ILR Press, 1989.

Toni Gilpin, Gary Isaac, Dan Letwin, and Jack McKivigan, <u>On Strike for Respect: The Yale Strike of 1984-85</u>, Charles H. Kerr Publishing Company, 1988.

Katherine Stone, "The Origins of Job Structures in the Steel Industry," in <u>Labor Market Segmentation</u>, by Richard C. Edwards, Michael Reich, and David Gordon, D.C. Heath, 1975.

I'll also add these two fascinating and long books that require a little more concentration:

E.P. Thompson, <u>The Making of the English Working Class</u>, Vintage Books, 1963.

Herbert Stein, The Fiscal Revolution in America, The University of Chicago Press, 1969.

Jean Fisher
Denver, Colorado, USA

Dear Jean,

"Class," like most words in English, can have many different meanings, and most discussions need first to clarify the *particular* meaning a *particular* word is expected to have in the *particular* discussion, or the discussion is likely to become a series of emotional dramatizations rather than a chance for rational communication. Mathematicians have learned to be quite careful about this step and the physical and biological sciences seem to be tending more and more in that direction if you look at the currently published scientific journals.

[Economists and political "scientists" who have to work in, fit into, and support the oppressive society for their livelihood are under considerable pressure to keep the smoke screen of confusion and multiple meanings of words going. This is necessary to avoid exposing either the reality of the society's and the economy's purpose (i.e., exploitation) or the utter illogic of their own theories.]

I would propose we settle for *two* different uses of the word "class" in our discussions of classism in RC and make plain each time we talk or write which meaning we are choosing.

The first meaning would be basic and would describe people's relation to the means of production. Here the *owning class* would be those people who own the means of production (the land, the forests, the mines, the factories, the banks, the railroads, the shops, the radio and television stations, etc.) and who buy the labor of non-owners and keep part of the value produced by these non-owners' labor for themselves. The only other basic class would be the non-owners, the *working class*, those people who sell their labor to the owning class and receive in return only a part of the value that their labor creates. "Middle-class" would describe a particular section of the working class, the workers who are granted special privileges and higher incomes in return for their managing and intensifying the exploitation of the other workers and for doing the intellectual labor, research, and education necessary for the economy to be profitable to the owning class.

The other possible use of the word "class" would be to describe particular groups of people who feel a common identity because of the particular roles they have been forced into, or have chosen, or have been assigned to within the operation of the two big classes. (Maybe even to label sets of patterns they have in common.) Here particular adjectives can be used to preface the word "class" and identify the group.

Some people have told me that they are comfortable with the label "raised poor class" as setting them distinct from their fellow working-class people whose parents had steady jobs. I have heard people describe themselves and others as "intellectual class," "farming class," "small storekeeping class," etc. One "preacher's kid" told me he came from the "clergy class."

Harvey Jackins

Speculating About What
Completely Rational Sexuality
Would Be Like For Humans

Earlier speculating on this topic, including the article *A Rational Theory of Sexuality*, has been useful. Co-Counselors attempting to re-evaluate their way through the huge amounts of confusing distress that the oppressive society has placed on the subjects of sex and sexuality have reported being reassured and assisted in discharging by these conjectures. We have come closer to general agreement as to what is rational in these areas. It is noticeable that the huge preoccupation with sexuality-related topics, which has been placed on most people in our cultures, has been noticeably reduced for most Co-Counselors.

There has come to be at least general agreement that almost all of the "guidelines" offered to us by the various cultures in the oppressive society have been distorted by various patterned biases. Partly as a result of this, a kind of a "tolerance" toward distressed sexuality has developed in the wide world. This has had its good side. A great shift away from the past persecution of people for their "differences" is noticeable among the general public although the old attitudes of oppression and mistreatment are still too dominant. Unfortunately the improved tolerance is often accompanied by an

Appeared in **Present Time** No. 88, July 1992.

"anything goes" attitude which is sometimes used as an apology and an excuse for sexist oppression and the sexual abuse of children. In the name of such tolerance, distressed behavior is often not only accepted, it is treated as if it were the only choice for the person with the distress.

Cultural conditioning has left most males, at least in Western cultures, with a *compulsive* drive towards, and *preoccupation with*, sex. On the other hand, women have been classically conditioned, with fears, warnings, shame, ridicule, and embarrassment, to be *inhibited* in the area of sex. Attempts have been made, by sections of the women's movement, to correct this obviously disadvantaging position. However, these attempts have often been geared to imitate the *male patterns* rather than to try to reveal and discover the actual inherent sexual nature of human *females*.

I have counseled a large number of individuals of both genders during all stages of the "sexual revolution," from 1950 to the present. In the process I think I have had some opportunity to glimpse what rational sexual functioning would be like if we could all become free from patterns in this area.

It seems clear to me that *rational sexual initiative and responsibility lies inherently with human females.* I think a rational population of both genders would quickly come to agreement on this. The basic motivation for sex is reproduction, for producing new human individuals, for guaranteeing the survival of the human race. Undistressed women inherently are deeply aware of this responsibility. Women's bodies furnish the ambience, the care, and the nourishment which make it possible for a fertilized ovum to become a human. Women are thoroughly committed to and in charge of the process as much as anyone except the fetus itself can be.

Women naturally nurse the newborn child, provide an over-whelmingly large share of the crucial early care, and are naturally set up to become the mentors, nurturers, counselors, and emotional supporters for the child most of the way to his or her adulthood.

Without any false information or distress patterns about sex, I think a well-informed woman would be free from any pulls, patterned or otherwise, to participate in sex *except when the natural functioning of her body would signal her of the opportunity for reproduction.* I suspect that a male human, free of patterns and conditioning, would, in a similar way, be uninterested in sex except upon receiving a signal from his female partner. (This seems to be true for other mammals and indeed for many other forms of life.)

My guess is that a rational woman (free of patterns) would be taking delight and pleasure in a great range of activities that have nothing to do with sex *until the actual time of ovulation.* Then the internal hormone shift would trigger an ancient inherited set of feelings of desiring sex. I think at such a moment the rational woman of the future would enjoy such a shift in feelings, feel reassured that her beautiful, complex body is working well, and would: (a) enjoy the feelings accompanying the change of hormonal state but not let that interfere in any way with the high priority activities in which she is engaged; or (b) decide quickly, based on past thinking and re-evaluation at the present moment that it is time to prepare for pregnancy by having uncontracepted sex; or (c) decide to carefully employ contraception to enjoy the recreational experience of helping and being helped to take pleasure in the feelings of sex and climax with someone whom she loves.

I think such a rational woman, having decided then or previously on who is the sexual partner of her choice, will inform such a partner of her desire, and that this, coming as the unprovoked choice of his female partner will in itself be the stimulus that "turns on" his interest, either in sex which leads to a pregnancy, or in recreational sex.

I suspect that once ovulation has finished, whether it has led to conception or not, the resulting hormone shift would return the attention of the woman to other affairs, whether these affairs are her usual adventures and preoccupations alone, or whether they now include these and the preparation for a thoroughly successful pregnancy.

In this happy kind of environment the present sexy calibre of most advertising would look completely ridiculous. It would be ineffective in selling people the goods they don't want in the hope for meeting frozen needs that can never be met.

I think children would know all about sex and could talk about it in simple language as soon as they bothered to ask questions.

I think there will be a great deal of touching and closeness between adults but which will only rarely, under the circumstances described above, lead to any sexual feelings or activity.

I think it will be very easy to arrange for zero population growth for our crowded world. This will be especially true when permission to have children will require graduation from courses involving the review and discharge of the distress from one's own childhood. I think commitments will be required of adults (who are seeking permission to become parents) that their planned one or two children have an organized prospect of being members of a group of close and friendly buddies with whom they play and learn all day. We have seen glimpses of the possibility of such arrangements in the kibbutzim of Israel, the progressive "creches" begun in the early years of the Soviet republics and in the happy preschools and primary grades of China in the early years following the Chinese liberation of 1949.

An Interview with Harvey Jackins

by Dorothy Carroll, the Editor of *Older and Bolder*

Older & Bolder: From your perspective, both as an International Reference Person and elder, how do you see the elders' movement outside RC and inside RC?

HJ: Inside RC I think it's very hopeful but not very powerful yet. It has had a few workshops, a few support groups, and a little discussion, but I think that in the main it has been dominated by clienting rather than by the sense of power that I think the elders need to take if they're going to play the role they should, and be a force in the general liberation movement. The possible numbers of participating elders is, of course, very large, and it is growing rapidly.

If elders do get themselves organized and come up with a good program and start being active, they can play a decisive role in many struggles that are going on. I think because of their greater experience, they can bring some clarity in places where people in other movements might tend to get confused.

There's a problem in that both inside RC and outside, the elders' movement is dominated by middle-class retirees who are concerned with their standard of living and having good vacations and leisure time. The great mass of elders who are living in intense poverty, which gets deeper and deeper as

Appeared in **Older and Bolder** No. 5.

the years go by, are not thought about well yet. I think the oppression is internalized to the extent that elders want to be taken care of a little bit and want to have comfortable chairs provided for them. In my opinion, of course, they should be leading everything. But I wouldn't say I have enormous support in this from other elders or other elder leaders in RC yet.

O&B: What are your thoughts on how the oppressions of classism and ageism intersect?

HJ: Well, classism is the basic oppression in our society, and it comes down hard on everyone, in that in general everyone produces far more value than they receive. The surplus is siphoned off to be wasted, spent as munitions, but also to make the too-wealthy people wealthier and wealthier. And this eventually leads to a breakdown in the economy, as we're experiencing now.

Basically every other oppression overlaps with classism because every other oppression is designed to make the oppressed person extra vulnerable to being exploited economically. So that the older you get, the more miserable your life is, unless you're one of the tiny group who actually owns more than you need for your living.

O&B: What is your thinking about ageism across the range of ages? What do you see as the differences and/or similarities between ageism for older people and what we used to call "adultism," now called the oppression of young people?

HJ: Well, every group that's oppressed is oppressed in every way they can be oppressed, and the motivation behind it, as I said above, is to exploit them more fiercely economically. The young people are fighting to get out of the under position; as they become adults, then in a sense they no longer suffer the oppression of young people, though they have a difficult time as young adults adjusting and learning how they're supposed to work.

Older people, on the other hand, are heading into what's often called the "nonproductive years." Unless they have very special economic circumstances, they begin to be short of what's needed to keep themselves alive. It's hard to have enough comfort, hard to pay for enough health care, and they become dependent and have to be taken care of by people in their family. Family members, even when they love the older people a great deal, find it an enormous burden to take care of them; they become impatient and it spoils the relationship. So I think those similarities are very plain.

O&B: How would you advise people of all ages, but particularly elders, to counsel on death and dying?

HJ: Well, as I have written and published, I don't think death is necessarily natural. The conditioning that has been put upon us with great distress—to accept death as inevitable—needs to be rejected. This is why in the commitment that I formulated, I said that "I solemnly promise I will never die and will never slow down, and will have more fun than ever." There are many scientific developments indicating that immortality might be possible for human beings just as it's already possible for single-celled animals. And so I would reject death as inevitable.

Most people have been made very frightened of death. It's a shock to young people when they first learn that death is regarded as inevitable. As far as I can tell, no young person ever was born with any other attitude than expecting to live forever.

People have worked in RC, sometimes for extended periods, on the assumption that they were immortal. They find that making this assumption is an extra contradiction to all kinds of distress and is very effective. In the wide world I have personally known quite a few people, who had met the danger of death in their lives so many times, either with illness or in battle, or in the hardships of life, that they had worn off their fears of death and were quite relaxed about it. As far as I can tell, I'm in that position now, too. It can very well be that I will die, but I will never agree to die. If death gets me it will be because it had to kill me in some way or other; it won't get me to yield.

I would set up contradictions to any acceptance of death. I would take all the actions I possibly could to keep one's health improving and improving and improving. I'm actually functioning better in my seventies than I did in my fifties. So, as you say, advise people of all ages, yes, but particularly elders, to get a motivation on you, so that when you hear the possibility of death snuffling around the corner of your house, you have already done a lot of the work and are already living each moment well.

O&B: Speaking personally, to what do you attribute your vitality and longevity, given the reality of your health? How do you use Co-Counseling in this regard?

HJ: Well, I think I would have been dead several times over if I had not discovered Co-Counseling and developed it, because I have been attacked by severe health crises all through my life. I had the 1918 flu and wasn't expected to live, and I have had innumerable surgeries and serious accidents. I have been beaten up. All the bones in my face were broken once.

What is responsible, I think, is that I had a good prenatal existence. My mother was my antagonist and almost my enemy from the moment I was born, but I think that she was healthy during the pregnancy and there was no threat of abortion or anything like that. It would have gone against her religious principles, so I think I had a good pregnancy and I was born expecting to have a hell of a good time. All the rejection that I've hit since has been hard, and it's slowed me down, but whenever I can get through a health crisis, or since counseling began—which is forty-two years now—whenever I've been able to turn a corner in my re-emergence, then I seem to bounce back. I recover.

Right now I'm very close to 150 pounds in weight. I was up to 200 at one time before my first heart attack. I have learned not to eat fats, with the help of Lisa Kauffman, a young doctor who gives me a lot of thoughtful information. I'm exercising and trying to keep on discharging everything I can dig out, which at this point is mainly a great amount of yawn stuff that interferes with my thinking. When I try to write an article and do some fresh thinking I soon simply fall asleep—I yawn for a long time and fall asleep and then wake up and start in again when I can. So that's all I'm doing.

O&B: In what directions would you like to see the elders' movement in RC move, develop, take off?

HJ: I would like to see the tough-nut leaders in RC, even if they're a little confused, (and of course they tend to be, like all of us), I would like to see them be forceful and organized and move on practical problems. The American Association of Retired Persons is mainly middle-class and is concerned with selling its members vacation packages and things like that, but it has an enormous membership, and I think there would be a great deal of room for RC elders to get in there, participate, and improve the programs.

As far as elders in RC, I think you need to go door-to-door and talk to a few people, get them together for an introductory lecture, and start some classes. Lots more of that is needed.

O&B: Do you have some special advice or directions you would like to give elders in RC to help us move in these directions?

HJ: Yeah. Get off your butts and move. The idea of sitting around and waiting to be cherished as an heirloom is exactly wrong. I don't think there's anybody else except us elders who has enough experience to be trusted with leadership. I think we should lead everything. Share it with everybody, but take the primary responsibility. Just like the good parents we were once upon a time, part of the time, anyway, we take responsibility for our family, which is all the people in RC and all the people we want to add to RC. Just move people. Educate them. Get them the theory. Help them get acquainted with it. And see that things happen. Take it on yourself to be the toughest, meanest leader there ever was.

O&B: Is there anything else you'd like to add?

HJ: Yes, I would like to pay a tribute to Elsie Darling for hanging in for so long to keep an elders' movement going. And to Finette Maloff for all the poems she wrote, and all the good humor she put into the difficult task of pulling stuff together, so that at this point the two tough East Coasters who have taken over, Marge Larrabee and Dorothy Carroll, can grasp the reins and build a tough movement. Let the elders become the dominant movement within RC, reaching for lots of women, because of the older people, women are the huge majority; and reaching for working-class people, who still stay practical a little longer than the ones who get stuck with middle-class issues.

I think elders should follow the organization plan we have for all liberation activities, which is that the Liberation Reference Person should see that City-wide Coordinators are set up for their group in every city where RC is active. Keep on the phone with them. Encourage them to get support groups started, and once there's one, get another support group started. Once there are two support groups, get the leaders together occasionally for a Wygelian leaders' meeting, and just spread enthusiasm and encouragement and enthusiasm and encouragement, and simply get the show on the road.

That's my proposal.

O&B: Thanks, Harvey, for your thoughts, inspiration, and kick-in-the-butt!

The Details and
History of
a Functioning
Organization

Prospects for RC:

Initial Report to the 1993 World Conference

As we meet at this 1993 World Conference, there are certain general topics that I propose we concentrate on. They are all interconnected, of course, by the reality of the Re-evaluation Counseling "movement," but they can usefully be looked at and discussed individually. These general topics are:

- The GROWTH of RC
- The UNITY of RC
- The STATE OF THE PRESENT SOCIETIES
- The RECLAIMING OF OUR POWER and the ATTAIN-MENT OF WIDER INFLUENCE
- The "NATURALIZING OF RC"
- PUBLIC RELATIONS
- The USE OF LITERATURE.

GROWTH

During the last four years, RC has expanded considerably in the geographical territories where it had previously established beginnings. There is new, significant activity at several locations in the former Soviet territories, especially around St. Petersburg, Yaroslavl, Ufa, Moscow, and the Baltic countries. There are new initiatives in the African population of

Appeared in **Present Time** No. 94, January 1994.

South Africa, and in several other African countries which were not yet involved at the time of the last World Conference. A small but firm beginning has continued in the People's Republic of China. The number of people involved in India has multiplied several times. Good beginnings are underway in several Latin American countries, in Central America, and in some Caribbean states. Geographical expansion has taken place in Australia, Spain, and Euskadi. Southeastern Europe has seen the establishment of Communities in Romania and Croatia, with some activity in Turkey and Iran.

Many existing Communities have expanded dramatically, with Regions dividing a number of times, and one Area often becoming two, three or four Areas.

The constituencies of **parents, young people, young adults, elders, disabled people, African heritage people, Latino/a heritage people, college** and **university faculty, artists, Asian heritage people,** and **raised-poor** and **working-class people** have all expanded greatly.

We are now reaching people who speak Arabic, Croatian, Finnish, Indonesian, Kiswahili, and Turkish.

We hope to establish an average growth rate for the number of RCers and for the number of Areas of *doubling each two years*. We hope to make persistent GROWTH a characteristic of all Community organizations.

We propose to require the teaching of at least one series of Fundamentals classes every year for an RC teacher to retain certification.

We propose to encourage Reference People to be bold in encouraging new teachers to try teaching, to not be timid in issuing one-time credentials to people who seem rationally committed to RC.

UNITY

Our Communities have remained remarkably united across the many geographical, language, and cultural barriers. In spite of our rapid growth, we have retained one world-wide leadership, one world-wide set of policies, and one growing theory, that is the same everywhere. Though many attacks have been launched at the Communities and at their leadership by reactionary forces from the oppressive society, these attacks have been largely rendered ineffective.

Conflicts engendered by "nationalism" have had no very serious effects within our existing Communities, even though they have been launched at RCers from outside forces. We have much more work to do in this regard since "national" and "patriotic" patterns are currently a principal tool of the oppressive societies in their efforts to foment conflicts and wars.

We have done well in handling and defeating a great variety of "attacks" on RC, on its theory, and on its leaders. We understand the patterns and mechanisms that give rise to these attacks much better than we did. However, we have much more to do in preparing our entire membership to be "attack proof."

A process for screening the people that we take into our classes and support groups needs to be spelled out and followed. A secondary screening for Co-Counselors who wish to claim the privilege of Community "membership" needs to be universally applied to safeguard our unity. At the same time, we need to be on guard that we do not use such screening unawarely to result in any prejudiced exclusion of any of the great varieties of people that belong in our Communities.

Present Time and the other journals play a key role in maintaining the unity of outlook which is so precious to RC and which makes it so effective. More thoughtful use of our literature and its wider distribution can defeat the divisiveness which the various agencies of the oppression continually attempt to foment among the population.

THE STATE OF SOCIETY

We have done well in raising the consciousness of our members and friends about the basically oppressive characteristics of the societies in which we live. Most RCers at present are aware that existing societies are largely patterned in their operation and oppressive in their effects upon us. Such consciousness-raising needs to be continued consistently.

Every particular oppression needs to be revealed to the liberation movements that are organized against it as based on and connected to the overall classist oppression on which present societies operate.

Insistent reminders that this society will inevitably collapse and is well on its way to such collapse need to be reinforced with encouragement to all RCers to take power, to take initiative, to take leadership in the replacing of this doomed structure with a rational set of world relationships.

THE RECLAIMING OF POWER AND
THE ATTAINMENT OF INFLUENCE

The reclaiming of power is at the heart of our re-emergence and needs continual exploration and demonstration in all of our counseling. This does not mean simply sitting back and criticizing the present state of affairs and proclaiming the desirability of a someday-to-be-attained just society. It means reaching for influence in *existing* organizations. It means getting actually involved in the process of furnishing effective leadership and encouragement to the people around us. The great majority of the populations among whom we live are being forced by the worsening of their lives into facing the need to struggle for themselves. Such struggles can be successful if the people involved are helped to reach effective policies.

THE "NATURALIZING" OF RC

The "naturalizing" of RC has been well-advanced in the last four years. We have delegates at this Conference who have been outstanding in this field. There is still much confusion among Co-Counselors generally, however, that "naturalizing" RC means "diluting" it, concealing the actual source of the ideas and policies, or treating RC as if it were something to be ashamed of or too dangerous to associate with. These patterned attitudes are nonsense and need to be exposed and eliminated.

We also need to learn how to better relate our wide world constituencies to our Community memberships. We need to create and master the transitions which will allow access to the full RC theory and practice to the wide worlders, and entrance into the Community for the most advanced people of the wide world. The RC Communities have operated during their first twenty-four years under a general agreement to avoid widespread publicity, to reach people individually, to treat participation in RC as a privilege rather than something to be "sold" to new people. Such publicity as we have participated in has often been forced upon us by attacks by government agencies, right-wing societies, or opportunistic reporters seeking a sensational topic to write about.

Our experience and our contacts have grown so substantially that the future may permit us to take more initiative. There is a widespread eagerness among the general populations for some reasonable thinking about the problems created by the oppression and the collapse of the society. Factual proposals or commentaries for and about the present crises in employment, in family life, in education, and in international relations are likely to find a thoughtful audience in this next period.

Probably the widespread distribution and sale of our books, pamphlets, journals and tapes will be a central channel for allowing the ideas of RC to circulate widely.

It is also time that we consider the choosing of responsible, experienced leaders of RC to appear at local, regional, or nation-wide forums, or even before the United Nations, as authorized spokespersons of the RC Community, offering a reasoned commentary and sensible proposals for the solution of the problems being considered.

The basic rule in the present *Guidelines* of no publicity on an Area level not first reviewed and approved by the Area Reference Person, and a similar constraint on any larger field of activity that requires the International Reference Person's approval, should stay in force. However, there are many, many leaders now capable of being delegated by the International Reference Person to speak out on controversial issues.

THOUGHTFUL, EFFICIENT USE
OF OUR LITERATURE

The preparation of our literature has been excellent from the beginning. Books, pamphlets, journals, brochures, lists of commitments, audio and video cassettes have all been prepared thoughtfully and with careful consultation with informed people. The quality of the thinking expressed in them and the breadth of the concerns they deal with has steadily improved and continues to improve.

Great care and devotion has been lavished on the technical excellence of our literature as well, and this has won widespread respect not only from readers in general but also from knowledgeable people in the editing and publishing professions. Almost every item that we have ever published is a permanent addition to the wealth of useful thinking that humanity has accumulated.

The distribution of our literature, however, is as yet only minimally successful. To the extent that we have distributed our literature well, it has played a major role in building our remarkable unity and the widespread respect afforded us by people who know of our existence. Yet only a small portion of RCers have as yet subscribed to *Present Time* (even!), though any person who reads our literature is always moved by the result. The determined, intensive circulation of our literature crucially needs attention, improvement and concentration.

There is a core group of RCers already in existence who are as enthusiastic, dedicated, and determined to improve literature circulation as are those of us who produce the literature. This core group simply needs to have its numbers multiplied ten times.

It is true that the patterns of "not reading" have been inculcated into almost the entire population by the misfunctioning of the schools in the last generation. It is almost certain that we will have to deal with this deliberately in our counseling of each other to make full use of the possibilities of heightened literacy.

Some leads already have been explored although not widely taken up and used. For example, almost every student in a Fundamentals counseling class who reads, prepares, and gives a report on an article from *Present Time*, becomes enthusiastic about the entire magazine and a loyal reader. When the leaders of an International Workshop distribute subscription blanks for *Present Time* at the beginning of a workshop and ask for them back with the subscription payment, the result is large numbers of new subscriptions. The new subscribers give every evidence of being pleased at having been so organized.

This World Conference can make a decisive difference to the circulation of our literature.

Two Successful
Continental Conferences

THE CONFERENCE FOR NORTH
AND SOUTH AMERICA

The second of the Continental Conferences scheduled for 1993 was held July 22-26 in Santa Fe, New Mexico, USA. It was very successful, with 118 RCers attending.

Delegates were invited and present from Mexico, Argentina, Trinidad, Montserrat, Canada, Barbados, Grenada, Guyana, El Salvàdor, Honduras, and the United States. International leaders for owning-class, middle-class, and young RCers were present from Ireland and England.

There were delegates from twenty-nine states of the United States and from four Canadian Provinces.

There were nine delegates present representing Native tribes and bands. There were thirteen people of African heritage, fifteen people of Latino/a heritage, and seventeen people of Jewish heritage. There were three people of Asian heritage, thirty-one men, and eighty-six women. There were substantial numbers of young people and young adults present. Working-class and raised poor people were about 55%, middle-class people 35%, and owning-class people 10% of the whole group.

Appeared in **Present Time** No. 93, October 1993.

Tim led a getting-acquainted and Co-Counseling work-shop the first two days.

Delegates reported on the state of their Regions and con-stituencies. Some new Regional Reference Persons and Inter-national Liberation Reference Persons were designated. RC journal editors met.

It was plain that tremendous growth had taken place on these continents (where RC first began and began to spread and where probably 75% of the world's Co-Counselors are still located).

There were many demonstrations of, and much practicing of, the Reality Agreement technique. This was uniformly intensely successful. Twenty delegates and six alternates were chosen for the World Conference in November, to be added to the four delegates chosen at the Australian Conti-nental Conference last January.

Charlotte Lowrey of Santa Fe, New Mexico, was the organ-izer.

THE CONFERENCE FOR AFRICA, THE MIDDLE EAST, AND EUROPE

The Conference for Africa, the Middle East, and Europe was held August 4-8, 1993, in Dublin, Ireland. It also was an outstanding success. Delegates were invited and present from Poland, Russia, England, Israel, Ireland, Sweden, Ro-mania, Belgium, Croatia, Finland, Hungary, Northern Ire-land, Luxembourg, Latvia, Germany, the Republic of South Africa, Austria, Norway, The Netherlands, Kenya, Zimbab-we, Denmark, Italy, Iran, Uganda, Spain, Estonia, France, Scotland, and Bashkiria. International leaders for African heritage people and for working-class people attended from the United States.

There was a strong delegation of eleven people from Africa, only one of whom was white. There was a strong delegation from the former Soviet areas. Together with a substantial group of African heritage people from England, these two caucuses contributed a great deal to the excitement and enthusiasm of the Conference. There were six delegates of Jewish heritage and one Arab. There were twenty-three men and fifty-five women. There were many young people and young adults.

The first day and a half was in this case also a get-acquainted and Co-Counseling workshop led by Tim. Much of the Co-Counseling in this workshop and in the Conference centered around the Reality Agreement approach, which worked successfully in every language in which it was attempted.

As in Australia and the Americas, delegates reported on the state of their Regions and constituencies, and there was great exultation at the enormous growth that had taken place since the last World Conference, both in the establishment of RC in additional countries and Regions, but also in the growth, strengthening, and the great increase in numbers in the previously active countries.

Twelve delegates were chosen to attend the World Conference in November.

Many delegates stayed over in Ireland and England as required by their airfares, visited, Co-Counseled, and some attended a working-class workshop in England led by Dan Nickerson.

Colette Morrison of Dublin, Ireland, was the organizer.

The Asian Continental Conference is taking place in October, and the World Conference will be held in November.

The July, 1992 International Leaders' Conference

An International Conference of RC leaders took place July 14th to July 21st, 1992, in Seattle, Washington, USA. They met to discuss the world situation, the current developments in RC, and to lay plans for the next period. A pre-Conference workshop took place from July 14th to July 17th to enable the people to become acquainted with each other, bring their counseling up-to-date, and get in some intensive counseling practice. This workshop was originally planned for leaders from the newer Communities, but all were welcome. One hundred people attended. It was led by Tim Jackins.

The Conference itself took place July 17th to July 21st and was led by Harvey and by Tim. All Regional Reference Persons and all International Liberation Reference Persons were invited to this Conference, as well as a number of "Chief Pioneers" in countries where RC is still in a developing stage.

One hundred and twenty people attended the Conference itself. They came from thirty-two different countries; twenty were people of color; twenty-seven were from countries where English is not the major language. There were twenty-nine men present, ninety-one women. There were sixty-five Regional Reference Persons present, thirty-four International Liberation Reference Persons, nineteen "Chief Pioneers."

Appeared in **Present Time** No. 89, October 1992.

Everyone functioned in support groups which met regularly. There were regular Co-Counseling sessions for everyone, both during the preliminary workshop and during the Conference itself. Wygelian Leaders' Groups of Regional Reference People from adjacent Regions of the earth alternated with Wygelian Leaders' Groups of International Liberation Reference People who led parallel or similar constituencies. The "Chief Pioneers" met in Wygelian Leaders' Groups to discuss the building of RC in their countries. There were many topic groups on liberation issues and scheduled meal table discussion groups at most meals. Reports from both kinds of discussions were made to the entire Conference.

Four principal classes took place. The first was on The Coming Changes In RC. The second was on Effective Counseling. The third was on Protecting and Correcting Leadership. The fourth was on Solving Problems.

There were several open question sessions. During these anyone could ask any other one of the hundred and twenty participants for information, help, encouragement, or "coaching."

In the last session of the Conference each person announced her or his plans for leadership in the coming period.

Summary of Harvey's Report on the Current Situation:

The world situation is very difficult for large numbers of people in every country in the world. The increasing collapse of the society is imposing intense hardships upon them. At the same time, the situation is favorable for action and for rational progress on the widest scale. People are ripe for change, starved for leadership, and ready to abandon much of the oppressive conditioning which they have been subjected to *if alternatives are offered to them.* The oppressive society's "solutions" to the problems of the people are being exposed as unworkable at a rapid rate. The claim that attempts to build a non-oppressive society will always fail because the Soviet beginnings in that direction had been betrayed and eventually abandoned in disarray, and because the Chinese leaders similarly are now trying to reinstitute capitalism, can easily be exposed. It is plain that the trouble in the Soviet and Chinese structures has been and is being caused by the persistence of oppressive patterns from the old societies in the heads of the Soviet leaders and, since Mao's death, in the heads of the dominant Chinese leaders. It is becoming plain that building a real non-oppressive society will require the use of the insights and practice of RC to remove the old society's patterns from people who take leadership in the new society.

The RC Community has been developing well. Putting together the main RC theory and developing a workable practice occupied the first twenty years. The last twenty-two and a half years, while continuing in the growth of theory and practice, have seen the spread of RC, largely by word-of-mouth, to the point that some kind of organized RC activity is now taking place in sixty-six countries.

Because the people coming into RC necessarily bring sets of already-accumulated patterns with them, almost everything that can possibly go wrong in a new Community usually does go wrong in the beginning periods. Many beginning Communities have "collapsed," but none of them has remained collapsed.

Workable *Guidelines* for the functioning of Co-Counseling and the Co-Counseling Communities have been carefully worked out and kept up-to-date for several years by now. The tendency of the Communities, however, has been to not follow the *Guidelines* carefully but to persist in various patterned habits of organization that they have borrowed from their experiences in the oppressive society. In the present period there is a noticeable tendency for this situation to be improved. The actual policies of the Community and the carefully-worked-out *Guidelines* are being taken more seriously and followed more carefully. In a number of places this is resulting in rapid, solid growth, the recruitment of new Co-Counselors of high quality, rapid advancement of new, excellent leadership, and the growth of new Areas and Regions through the division of existing ones.

The past level of functioning of RC has been good enough and successful enough that we can all take pride in it. It is time, however, for a much more careful, vigorous growth, using the knowledge that we have accumulated. It is time for *all* classes, *all* Areas, *all* support groups, *all* Regions, *all* Wygelian Leaders' Groups to grow and expand continuously.

Even functioning as sloppily as we have tended to do in the past, RC has persisted and grown and rooted itself deeply in a wide variety of populations, language groups, and liberation constituencies. To actually responsibly and carefully *use* the knowledge and theory and organizational practice we have accumulated, will lead to vigorous growth in the near future.

From one point of view we have done very well. If events in the world were only taking place at the same moderate speed as our improvement and functioning, we could be quite relaxedly pleased. Instead, however, the dangers facing the world's people from the collapse of the society are *very* real and potentially *very* damaging. Actually *millions* of people are facing starvation under the bungling nationalism, profiteering, and war-mongering of the collapsing society. The

AIDS pandemic can actually wipe out half of the world's population if it is not handled better than the way the oppressive society is currently dealing with it. The blighting of the younger generation, a continuing anti-human process for the last 6,000 years, is currently being intensified to effectively destroy large numbers of our brightest and most promising humans.

I propose to this Conference that we not only take pleasure in the undoubted achievements of RC, that we not only bring our Communities up to elegant functioning and continued growth, but also that we take a third decisive step. I propose that we "extrude" an entirely new level of activity of RCers, an entirely new layer of people who will become responsible, powerful, and confident enough to take charge of the entire environment and see that a rational future for all humans is organized.

How shall a large group of our people transcend the best functioning that we have previously attained? How can we assist each other to "take charge of everything"? How can we change ourselves from being devoted "supporters of" and "well-wishers to" into initiators, "requirers," sources of confidence, and triumphant achievers of desirable, rational change?

I think seeking answers to these questions brings us up against a barrier that we have been aware of and have been trying to find a solution to for a long time. This is the unsolved-until-now reclaiming of our individual, total power. We have convincing reasons to believe that every one of us possessed this power and still possesses it inherently. We have assumed that what has been standing in the way of this inherent power must be "powerlessness patterns." We have speculated as to why we have not been able to see such patterns clearly, why we have not been able to find dependable contradictions that work consistently, and why no substantial breakthroughs against these barriers have occurred.

It now seems certain that pursuing the "I can and I will" commitment against specific barriers will either solve this problem or reveal any further actions that will need to be taken to solve it. (Almost any client who has made substantial early progress in her or his counseling finds herself or himself discharging if she or he determinedly promises and re-promises that "I CAN [do something that I greatly desire to accomplish] and I WILL.")

Part of the work of the Conference will consist of demonstrations with people towards taking total power and total responsibility for the straightening out of the entire world. Typically, as you will see, the client engaging in the challenge to the presumed powerlessness patterns will discharge extremely well and will then tend to shift her or his attention to an important chronic pattern from which she or he wishes to be free. As they discharge on that you will observe them being pulled to narrow their contradiction to dealing only with that pattern, not with the entire problem of powerlessness. You will see that keeping the wording of the commitment to challenging the powerlessness itself, however, works even better than contradicting the particular chronic pattern. I think you will observe strong indications that it is important for the client to resist this pull (apparently arising from the powerlessness pattern itself) to shift the client's effort to contradict toward a less difficult distress.

This is the three-point program of the 1992 International Leaders' Conference:

(1) Take pride and satisfaction in the already-won achievements of the Re-evaluation Counseling Community, its theory, and its organization, and take heart and confidence for the future from these achievements of the past;

(2) Reorganize our existing Communities cleanly and efficiently. Use the hard-won knowledge, as embodied in the *Guidelines*, of how Co-Counselors can work well together. Make continual growth and the prompt solving of difficulties a channel for spreading the insights of RC until they are clearly available everywhere in the world;

(3) Create a new layer of RCers and RC activity (to which everyone is welcome to aspire). This group of people will take responsibility for, reach for, and assume power in handling *all* difficulties in the world, not only in the RC Communities, not only in local or regional environments, but everywhere, regardless of their own geographical or social locations.

Bringing Our Organization Up to Date

All of us have a personal stake in enlarging the numbers of RCers in the world. All of us will gain generally by improving the connection of the RC Communities with ourselves.

The growth of RC is intellectually satisfying. We naturally take pleasure in the gains of others. More immediately important is that having a larger number of people share our insights increases the safety of our lives. It enhances our ability to attain even our most personal goals.

We have often lost sight of this because of our common patterns and traditions of isolation. We have become distracted by the crises threatened by the collapsing society. Many of us have settled, temporarily, for a limited, formal participation in RC. We have "used" but have not "built" a local Community. We have settled for "stability" rather than growth. Some new RCers have gotten the impression from our attitudes that the present level of functioning of our local Community is satisfactory.

We can be pleased with the state of functioning which Co-Counseling and the Communities have managed to achieve in spite of the tolerated sloppiness and confusion so far, but we cannot afford to be satisfied with it. Receiving full benefits from the insights of RC requires continual GROWTH. If every RC group or organization to which we belong is not

Appeared in **Present Time** No. 90, January 1993.

growing and extending continuously, we are letting ourselves be cheated.

We possess a set of policies and practices, mostly but not entirely summarized in the *Guidelines*, of how the RC Communities and their various organizations can work *well*. The *Guidelines* and the other policies have been worked out from much discussion and out of many years experience. It is a mistake to allow parts of the *Guidelines* to slip into disuse. When we do this, we slide back into conducting RC activities and relationships in the ways of the oppressive society.

Most "old ways of doing things" did not work well. They were usually part of some oppressive scheme in the society. The organizational thinking of the past was almost entirely patterned. In the many revisions of the *Guidelines* most of this contamination from the past had been eliminated. Successful experiments with more rational organizational forms had taken place.

Examine the neighborhood organizations of the Community. A fully Organized Area of the Community has a key functionary known as the Area Reference Person (there is also an already-designated replacement for the ARP in case of emergency, the Alternate Area Reference Person).

There was, when the Communities first started, an understandable tendency to turn the Area Reference Person, whose intended role was that of exercising judgment on a small number of organizational questions, into a "key executive officer" who "led" on all questions, who dominated the work of the Area, and who acted authoritatively and with finality. With such expectations from the members some Area Reference Persons responded with just such rigid functioning and "modelled" in that ineffective direction. Some of them accomplished Community growth in spite of the way they went about it. It was at the cost, however, of great effort. It also tended to exclude most of the members of the Area from the experiences of leadership which should have been open to them.

For several years now it has been *official* policy to put leadership functions in the hands of leaders' groups (Wygelian leaders' groups) with a carefully-thought-out "Wygelian" agenda. *It has been policy* to depend for the growth of the neighborhood Communities on such meetings of small groups of people who live near each other. If these groups meet *occasionally* to discuss and plan how to enlarge RC where they live, they will almost certainly recruit nearby residents for support groups and classes. This will lead to this portion of an Area growing to Area size. If the neighborhood group is outside an existing Area, it will become a fast-growing nucleus for a "new" Area.

Who should see to it that such meetings take place? Any and every RCer is inherently in charge to see that this happens, to initiate and remind and encourage and congratulate the process as it takes place. If no one else begins it, certainly the Regional Reference Person (or the International Liberation Reference Person in the case of non-geographical groupings) will. Once begun there will be a need for more Consultants for such groups than one person can fill, so short classes can be organized by the first initiator to train people to function as such Consultants. Such training and experience will enhance the confidence and enthusiasm (and the initiative) of the ones who participate.

A Wygelian leaders' group for Regional leaders needs to meet occasionally in every Region. No Regional Reference Person should be expected to function by herself or himself.

The same should be true for the leaders around an International Liberation Reference Person or his or her deputy on a Regional level.

Every Area Reference Person needs a Wygelian leaders' group meeting with her or him occasionally. Every group with common functions needs to be led the same way. There will be Wygelian leaders' groups on an Area level for RC teachers, for assistant RC teachers, for support group leaders, for workshop organizers, for literature agents plus newsletter workers plus introductory lecturers.

Functioning up-to-date like this with the idea of growth in mind will let our Communities surge ahead in numbers and effectiveness. The individual benefits to each of us will surge at the same pace.

Rules for Scheduling, Leading, and Accounting for RC Workshops (Reminder)

(Some carelessness has recently crept into the organizing, scheduling, and accounting of some RC workshops. There are definite rules about these. The rules have been worked out as a result of much experience. These rules must be followed unless permission for deviation from them for a particular workshop has been received, *in advance,* from the International Reference Person.)

ALL WORKSHOPS NEED TO BE APPROVED <u>IN ADVANCE</u> BY THE RESPONSIBLE REFERENCE PERSON
(An RC teacher may schedule a workshop *for the members of her or his class only* without anyone else's approval.)

Workshops that include Co-Counselors within one organized Area but for more than one teacher's students must have the approval of the Area Reference Person. If there is no Area Reference Person, the workshop must have the approval of the Regional Reference Person. If there is neither an Area Reference Person nor a Regional Reference Person, permission should be secured from the International Reference Person.

Appeared in **RRP** No. 10, 1994.

Workshops that are open to and limited to Co-Counselors within a particular Region must have the approval of that Regional Reference Person.

A workshop which invites Co-Counselors from a particular constituency (women, men, young adults, working-class people, etc.) should be approved *in advance* by the International Liberation Reference Person of that constituency (or in the case of a Regional or Area workshop, by the City-wide or Region-wide Coordinators who are deputies of that International Liberation Reference Person). This is in addition to approval by the geographical leadership.

If workshops for a previously unorganized category or constituency of Co-Counselors are being initiated, the International Reference Person's approval must first be secured.

EXCEPT FOR WORKSHOPS FOR ONE TEACHER'S STUDENTS, THE LEADERS OF WORKSHOPS IN ALL LEVELS AND CATEGORIES MUST BE APPROVED BY THE RESPONSIBLE REFERENCE PERSONS UNDER WHOSE SUPERVISION THEY LEAD

The leadership of workshops on an Area or neighborhood level must be approved by the Area Reference Person. The leadership of workshops reaching to people within one Region must be approved by the Regional Reference Person where one exists, or by the International Reference Person. The leadership of workshops inviting people outside organized Areas or more widely than one Region must be approved by the International Reference Person. Individuals who wish to lead workshops outside their own Area but within their own Region must have the approval of the Regional Reference Person to do so where a Regional Reference Person exists, or of the International Reference Person.

Persons who wish to lead workshops outside their own Region must have the prior approval of the International Reference Person *for each such workshop.*

WORKSHOPS ARE LED BY *ONE* LEADER AND ORGANIZED BY *ONE* ORGANIZER EXCEPT BY SPECIAL PERMISSION OF THE INTERNATIONAL REFERENCE PERSON. LEADERSHIP FEES ARE PAID ONLY TO *ONE* LEADER. ORGANIZERS' FEES ARE PAID TO ONLY *ONE* ORGANIZER. IF THE LEADER USES ASSISTANTS OR THE ORGANIZER USES ASSISTANTS, THEY ARE EITHER VOLUNTEERS AND UNPAID, OR PAID BY THE INDIVIDUAL LEADER OR ORGANIZER OUT OF HIS OR HER FEE AT HIS OR HER CHOICE.

ALL WORKSHOPS (AT EVERY LEVEL) SHALL CONTRIBUTE TEN PERCENT OF THE GROSS INCOME OF THE WORK-SHOP ("OFF THE TOP") TO THE COMMUNITY SERVICE FUND OF PERSONAL COUNSELORS INC. FOR COMMU-NITY-SERVICING AND INTERNATIONAL OUTREACH. THERE ARE NO EXCEPTIONS TO THIS REQUIREMENT, AND THE PLANNING AND ACCOUNTING FOR THE WORK-SHOP MUST INCLUDE THIS.

Scholarships to the workshops for workshop fees, or for transportation expenses, may be furnished only from the official Outreach Funds (Area or International) of the Community and not from the workshop funds themselves.

The maximum daily fee for leading a workshop has been set as follows:

- For International Reference Persons—$750 a day
- For Regional Reference Persons or International Liberation Reference Persons—$300 a day
- For Area Reference Persons—$200 a day
- For RC teachers—$100 a day.

These are maximum fees, and a lower fee may be negotiated with the leader. (The fees are frequently lowered or waived by leaders developing new Communities.) A Friday evening to Sunday afternoon workshop counts as two days.

The leader's fare to the workshop shall be paid.

Workshops organized on an Area or class level shall divide the income left after expenses (the term "expenses" to include the basic fees agreed upon for the leader and for the organizer of the workshop) between the leader and the Community Service Fund of Personal Counselors Inc., one-quarter to the leader and three-quarters to the Community Service Fund of Personal Counselors Inc. Three-tenths of this three-quarters shall be used for servicing the Community and for International Outreach. Seven-tenths of these amounts (the three-quarters of net income) may be withdrawn for local outreach purposes on signed, approved applications by the Area Reference Person (or designated teacher in an unorganized Area) to the Community Service Fund of Personal Counselors Inc.

In the case of Regional and International level workshops, the leader shall receive, in addition to his or her regular fee, one-fourth of the *net* income from the workshop. The organizer's basic fee shall be negotiated between the organizer and the leader but shall not exceed one-fourth of the leader's basic fee. The organizer shall receive one-twelfth of the *net* income. Personal Counselors Community Service Fund (International Outreach) shall receive one-third of the net, as shall the Publications Fund of Rational Island Publishers, Inc.

Any exceptions to the above rules must be approved in advance by the International Reference Person. This includes such special cases as Family Workshops where more than one leader is necessary or workshops where special expenses for physical assistance, translation, etc. are necessary.

APPROVAL OF THE INTERNATIONAL REFERENCE PERSON MUST BE SECURED IN ADVANCE FOR ANY DEVIATION FROM THESE RULES.

Do *Not* Recruit Co-Counselors Into Wide-World Organizations Which You Are Leading or Building

Leaders in RC are expected, whenever possible, to extend leadership to, and help work out policy for, wide-world liberation movements which have rational programs moving in the same direction as RC liberation movements. RCers are encouraged, once they have become clear enough and able enough to do so, to play a role in supporting wide-world organizations which embrace people of their own constituency and which have progressive and liberating policies.

Where such organizations do not already exist in the wide world, RCers are encouraged to assume leadership in organizing them and guiding them.

Many years ago we decided to recommend a policy of "balanced leadership," of a leader "having one foot in the RC Communities and one in the wide world and leading effectively in both."

As a result of these policies, thousands of RCers have become effective activists in many progressive organizations.

Appeared in **RRP** No. 10, 1994.

A growing number of RCers have joined existing liberation organizations dealing with women's liberation, men's liberation, children's liberation, parents' liberation, young people's liberation, young adults' liberation, the elimination of racism, the elimination of classism, and many more.

A certain number of effective RC leaders have launched new organizations for taking the key elements of liberation policies as worked out within RC to the wider public. Learning as they go, some have built fine organizations with substantial memberships which bring progressive policies or "naturalized RC policies" to large numbers of enthusiastic people.

When this organizing and expansion of wide-world organizations by RC leaders first began, I was slow to recognize the possibility of difficulties arising out of the participation of other RCers in organizations formed and led by RC leaders. I was concerned about getting started in these directions and finding out what was possible. I did not recognize that there would be a temptation facing the initiating leader to "borrow" some other RCers to assist him or her, who were seen as "already committed" and "knowledgeable" in the particular field of liberation, and therefore tempting as a "short cut" around the job of educating and training members and leaders for the wide-world organization. I did not recognize that this was a serious violation of the "no socializing" principle which had been found necessary in other relations between RCers. I failed to see that it involved setting up a second relationship with a person when the existing relationship was based on both people being Co-Counselors in their primary relationship, that they "knew each other" because of their existing membership in the Co-Counseling Community.

Some of you RC leaders launched new organizations which succeeded and continue to be successful but "borrowed" other RCers to help you and to share leadership in the wide-world organization. In the beginning, some of you leaders consulted me about "recruiting" other RCers to lead portions of your wide-world organizations in the places where they were residents or where they had a particular interest in the policies. Some of you did not consult me but simply went ahead with such recruiting. When the "need" of the leader for "experienced assistants" was offered as a reason for recruiting RCers, I did not firmly require a correct policy. I was too "eager" to help see that the wide-world organizational efforts were successful. I yearned to see models of correct dual leadership where you were leading both in RC and in wide-world organizations.

I was wrong in this. Such actions should not have taken place. I apologize to the Community for these lapses in judgment.

Some of you have complained to me that people that you have trained to become leaders of RC, and have made considerable investment in their training, have been "recruited" by others of you who are leading wide-world organizations to assist them (without any consultation with you who had found and developed these people). Often, apparently, the jobs in the wide-world organizations seemed "easier" than the jobs you had planned to train them to take in RC. Sometimes, you have said, the more substantial financial incomes that seemed possible in the wide-world organizations were too tempting (in today's shaky economy) for the recruited people to give balanced consideration to the opportunities for their development as RC leaders which you had planned.

For now I do not propose that we be "retroactive" in undoing what has already taken place. I ask that the people who have been involved in these mistakes think carefully about how to correct policy with (hopefully) as little disruption of people's lives and functioning as possible.

It is simply time to re-assert and apply the no-socializing principle of the *Guidelines* to *all* the relationships which might occur between RCers in wide-world work.

The relationship of Co-Counselors in or leading wide-world organizations to other Co-Counselors should be governed by the following principles:

1. Co-Counselors in or leading wide-world organizations should not recruit other Co-Counselors into their organizations. If other Co-Counselors ask to join their wide-world organizations, these other Co-Counselors should instead be urged to start their own wide-world organizations and recruit contacts from the wide world, rather than "huddle" with people who have already been organized.

2. Co-Counselors should not *hire* other Co-Counselors to work in their wide-world organizations. They should train people from their wide-world organizations to do the leading. In practice they will need to teach such people RC or bring them to RC classes and other RC activities for the training in RC which they will need to become maximally effective leaders.

3. Institutions (governments, schools, colleges, hospitals, etc.) often need the intervention of some of the effective wide-world organizations which are being led by Co-Counselors. Co-Counselors in these institutions may invite these organizations into their institution to do particular workshops or

training (just as they may invite the RC Community in to teach RC classes) for the members of the institution. However, the Co-Counselor arranging for such an invitation is acting *for the institution* and should not take charge of the activity of the wide-world organization within the institution.

4. Co-Counselors who have organized or become leaders in wide-world organizations should keep in mind that training and encouraging training of the members of their wide-world organizations and offering them the perspective of joining the RC Community will be helpful to these members learning to lead well.

5. If Co-Counselors are leading wide-world organizations, they have a responsibility to their members to make *full knowledge of RC* available to these people and not limit them to a diluted or incomplete version of it. (*Naturalizing* RC does not mean diluting it or communicating only fragments of it.) People will need it *all* as the struggle to end all oppressions and advance humanity progresses.

6. RCers who lead wide-world organizations need to remember that they can always, in every situation, *think* as RCers and think of spreading our precious information as widely as possible.